The Z brand came to Arizona from Texas with John Slaughter in 1879. He registered it and ran it on the right shoulder of his livestock at the old San Bernardino (Slaughter) Ranch in southeast Arizona.

Marion Williams, my grandfather, bought the ranch and the brand from Slaughter in 1937. He used the brand until his death in 1963, and it then passed to the author, who uses it for livestock–and the Smokin' Z Press.

• • •

In Ben Williams' new book, Pancho Villa–A Lifetime of Vengeance, the infamous revolutionary weaves his evil heart in and out of an American family tapestry, in which author Ben F. Williams, Jr. spins the tales of his own boyhood years growing up in the southeastern corner of Arizona and Sonora, Mexico. Through facts and memorable reality from his parents and life-long friends, Williams' stories follow the crazed Pancho Villa from his earliest days of life, through war and survival along the border lands. Williams includes horrific tales of Villa's famous battles and his growing eccentric and violent behavior, as personal cruelty and murders increase.

This well-researched book culminates with little-known truths about the disappearance of Pancho Villa's skull . . . from his grave in Parral, Mexico.

In his third book, Ben F. Williams, Jr., discloses a wealth of information about what it was like for a boy and his family to ranch, mine, and survive during Mexican revolutionary times. Against this background, he not only tackles stories about Pancho Villa's battles and the man accused of stealing Villa's skull from his grave, but he baits the reader with the most curious story of all: Who was the accused thief of the skull, Emil Holmdahl? What was his connection to Ben F. Williams, Sr.–the author's father? And where is Pancho Villa's skull today?

PANCHO VILLA

A Lifetime of Vengeance

Ben F. Williams, Jr. (signature)

Ben F. Williams, Jr.

Smokin Z Press   Tucson, Arizona

This edition was prepared for printing by
Ghost River Images
5350 East Fourth Street
Tucson, Arizona 85711
www.ghostriverimages.com

Edited by Elizabeth Ohm

Cover photograph courtesy of
C.L. Sonninchsen Special Collections Department
University of Texas at El Paso Library

ISBN 978-0-9794800-2-7

Library of Congress Control Number: 2010914119

Printed in the United States of America

First Printing: October, 2010

10 9 8 7 6 5 4 3 2 1

Dedication

This book is dedicated lovingly to my grandchildren,
Beth, Katy, Kathleen, Kristin, Natalie and Pierce.

Author's Note

While on vacation in July of 2009, I read *An American Family–The Buckleys*, by F. Reid Buckley. The book contained a description of Pancho Villa, who was personally well known to the senior Buckley. Struck by his description of Villa, I wrote a story. The story led to another, which in turn drove me to yet another, and before I knew it, I had written this book.

Learning of my family's connection to the events of the Mexican revolutions and Villa, I decided to weave those stories into the fabric of this book–stories about Villa, the Williams family, and Mexican revolutionary days.

NOTE: Endnotes in this book are indicated by numbers in parentheses, i.e. (1), (2), etc.

Acknowledgements

In acknowledging the people whose efforts and talents contributed to this book, I must first gratefully thank my very capable assistant, Marilyn Bender. Marilyn's abilities at organizing, typing and editing have made it possible to produce this collection of stories.

Many thanks to my wife, Daisy, who patiently read and listened to my stories, too many times. Thanks also to my children, Liz, Diane, Kate, and Ben III, who helped with research and initial editing.

I also appreciate the contributions of many others who have helped me with this book: My highly capable and perceptive editor, Elizabeth Ohm. Penny Porter, a skilled and fine author of many books and published stories, who provided a number of wonderful ideas for this book. Katherine Reeve, Bruce J. Dinges, and Dave Thackenburg, at the Arizona Historical Society. Danny Gonzalez, El Paso Public Library–Border Heritage Center. Laura K. Hollingsed and Yvette N. Delgado, C.L. Sonnichsen Special Collections, University of Texas at El Paso Library. Elizabeth Ames, Cochise County Historical Society. Armando Elías, good friend, prominent author, and historian. Henry Zipf, colleague and life historian. Cindy Hayostek, author and historian. Ben T. Traywick of Tombstone, Arizona, prominent historical author. Frank and Beverly Collins, owners of The Good Egg restaurants in Tucson, and their manager, Nathan Arndt. The Pima County Public Library. Stefano "Steve" Corradini. Stephen M. Brophy.

Roberto Ruiz. Licenciado Francisco Arturo Lizarraga Garcia. José Castellanes of Agua Prieta, Sonora. My cousin Tooter's wife, Betty Williams. Jack Riddle and Annie Larkin, Bisbee Mining & Historical Museum. Harvey Finks, Johnson Historical Museum of the Southwest. My colleagues in the Quail Run and Saturday writing groups.

If I have omitted anyone from this list, I apologize. It is an innocent oversight.

Contents

Dedication
Author's Note
Acknowledgements
Other books by Ben F. Williams, Jr.

Other books by Ben F. Williams, Jr.

Tales of My Southwest

More Tales of My Southwest

1

PANCHO VILLA RIDES INTO OUR LIVES

Pancho Villa rode . . . from Durango to Parral, and on the way into the path of the Williams family.

Born in Durango, killed in Parral, who really was Pancho Villa?

Villa's first encounter with our family took place on Tuesday morning, August 31, 1914. My father, Ben F. Williams, Sr., was washing Granddad Marion's new Franklin air-cooled touring car on the front lawn of the Williams home on Seventh Street in Douglas.

Granddad's Franklin touring car

Ben, Sr., then thirteen years old and in the eighth grade, was surprised when his next-door neighbor, Francisco Elías, approached.

Wealthy and influential, Elías owned a ranch in Sonora as well as a home on Seventh Street. He would become governor of Sonora, then Secretary of Agriculture in the cabinet of Mexican President Elías Calles, whose term of office was from 1924 to 1928.

Francisco Elías gained fame and reputation in later years. When asked to report on possible un-American activities of Hilario Gabilondo, Rafael Gabilondo, and Rafael Gabilondo, Jr.,(1) who were requesting U.S. passports, the U.S. Bureau of Investigation (forerunner of what was later to become the FBI) issued an inside confidential report in November 1918, which said, among other things, that "the Gabilondo family is wealthy. They together with the Elías family, of whom General Calles is a member, virtually control Sonora. They form what the Mexicans call the Inner Circle in Sonora politics. It is more than possible that the state [Sonora] could be handled through the people named above. Rafael Gabilondo speaks English and is associated in business with Alfred Paul."(2)

This report covers the years 1914 to 1915 when Mexican revolutionary and federal forces were at each other's throats. The report was only recently declassified and made available for public viewing.

When Francisco Elías approached my father, he asked, "Ben, do you know how to drive this car?" pointing to the Franklin sedan.

"Yes, Don Francisco, I can drive this car."

"Good. I have to go to the depot to meet the train and my car won't start. Pancho Villa and his staff are coming to Douglas and they are expecting me to drive them around town. Can you do it?"

"Of course," young Ben eagerly responded.

The two got into the car, and Ben drove to the train depot. They arrived at the station just as the train pulled in. Villa and nine of his

Ben F. Williams, Sr., age 13, when he drove Pancho Villa in the Franklin touring car

pistoleros (bodyguards) climbed into and onto the Franklin–with Villa, Elías, and young Ben in the front seat. Three bodyguards rode in the back seat, and three rode on each running board, their combined weight causing the vehicle to ride on its axles.[1]

Dad chauffeured the group around Douglas, and then later in the evening took them to a Chamber of Commerce dinner at the Douglas Golf Club, where Villa, the self-proclaimed governor of Chihuahua, was the guest of honor.(3)

---

1 On the train with Villa was General Obregón, later to become militarily famous and president of Mexico from 1920 to 1924. Obregón lost his right arm in the Battle of Celaya, where he defeated Villa in April 1915.

On that day, Villa gave Granddad a passport issued by him which granted permission for Granddad to come and go through Chihuahua. Permission was also authorized in the passport for Marion Williams to cross through Villa's army lines without being questioned or detained.

It wasn't the last time the Williams family would run into Villa.

Marion owned and operated the Santa Rosa Ranch ten miles northwest of Nacozari, Sonora. The ranch was well stocked with more than 1,500 head of cattle. During a Villa military campaign in Sonora, one of Marion's cowboys rode his horse to the ranch house to inform Granddad that a military detachment was rounding up 300 head of cattle to take to Villa's camp outside of Nacozari to feed his troops.

Upon hearing the cowboy's story, Granddad saddled his horse and rode out to meet Villa's detachment. Approaching the captain in charge of the detail, Granddad challenged him. "You

Mexican corriente cattle

14

know those cattle are mine. If you take them, I'll have no choice but to resist. Why don't you go to my neighbor's ranch? He's an American by the name of Sherman who has left the country. He's back somewhere in Kansas, hasn't been here in months. Take 300 from his herd . . . and we won't have to fight."

The captain, seeing an easy way out of a sticky situation, said "*Muy bien*," and ordered his soldiers to take Sherman's cattle instead of Granddad's.

Before Villa's attack on Agua Prieta, the United States military had positioned artillery units in the foothills northeast of Douglas, overlooking Agua Prieta. Their commanding officer sent word to the Mexicans that if there was any fighting or shelling by Mexicans on American soil, his artillery–already in position–would decimate Agua Prieta in an artillery barrage that would leave that city's adobe brick buildings crumbling in the dust.

During the Agua Prieta attack, bullets found their way into and around Douglas where residents, including youngsters, climbed atop rooftops and railroad cars to watch the battle.

Dad, along with others, watched the two-day battle from the roof of the Gadsden Hotel in Douglas.

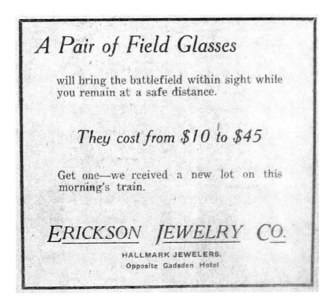

Ad for binoculars, to view the battle of Agua Prieta, October 1915, *Douglas Daily Dispatch*. Courtesy of Arizona Historical Society

2

WHO WAS PANCHO VILLA?

In order to better appreciate the Mexican revolutions, we must visit the early days of Pancho Villa, who was to become a national hero and a person of international fame. Villa gained notoriety in the early 1900s, and stories about the revolutionary giant continue to the present day.

Not only did Villa carry out military campaigns in northern and central Mexico, at one time he shared the "presidential chair" in Mexico City with Emiliano Zapata, a popular and capable revolutionary leader from southern Mexico.

The person we know as Pancho Villa literally lost his head as a consequence of the revolution in which he played a dominant and commanding part. To better understand what made him tick, a review of his origins is in order.

There have been numerous and differing stories written about when, where, and to whom the bandit was born. Much has been written of his exploits, but there seems to be great confusion and lack of information regarding his origins.

People have come to know the name Doroteo Arango as being synonymous with Pancho Villa. The date of birth, place of birth, and the name of Pancho Villa, although written about by many, were really for the most part no more than educated guesses, suppositions, and even some fictitious images. Following is one version that has been widely accepted.

Christened Doroteo Arango, Villa was born in San Juan del Rio, Durango, Mexico, on June 5, 1878. His adoptive father died when he was twelve, leaving him as head of the family with two younger brothers and two sisters, whom, along with his mother, he supported.

Villa killed his first man while a teenager. The victim was the son of a *hacendado* (landed squire) who purportedly had raped Villa's sister, Mariana. Some historians and writers allege that the perpetrator was the old hacendado himself.

By the time he was twenty, Arango had become a veteran outlaw, attaching himself to a band of which a man called Pancho Villa was chieftain. When the bandit chief was killed, twenty-year-old Doroteo Arango adopted his name, striking out on his own with several members of the old gang. Doroteo Arango became Pancho Villa–a name he blazed into history.

Rubén Osorio, a Mexican with at least three published books in recent years, set out to determine for himself Villa's origins and background. He also wanted to find out what shaped Villa's personality and molded the legendary leader of the "Division of the North"–the acclaimed "centaur of the north."[2]

Pancho Villa in 1899, at age 22. Unknown photographer

---

2 The *American College Dictionary* defines "centaur" as "one of a race of monsters having the head, trunk, and arms of a man, and the body and legs of a horse."

To determine the true origin and background of his subject, Osorio traveled through the Mexican countryside in the states of Chihuahua, Durango, Mexico, Coahuila, and Jalisco. During his travels, Osorio spent 300 hours interviewing 28 different individuals. His information revealed that when Villa married Luz Corral at the church in San Andrés, Chihuahua, he signed the matrimonial record as Francisco Villa from San Juan del Rio, Durango, son of Augustín Villa and Micaela Arámbula. (Parochial Archive of San Andrés, Chihuahua, contains a marriage act between Luz Corral Fierro and Francisco Villa dated May 27, 1911.)

While interviewing Dr. Camacho Fermán in Chihuahua City in 1986, Osorio was greatly surprised when Dr. Fermán told him:

"It is an oral tradition in my family that Doroteo Arango, or Francisco Villa, was the illegitimate son of my great-grandfather, Don Luis Fermán, a hacendado of Jewish-Austrian origin. He arrived in Mexico in the middle of the last century [1800s] from the principality of Liechtenstein, and took up roots in Durango."

Dr. Fermán went on to relate that in the middle of the nineteenth century, Luis Fermán lived in Schaan, a small industrial city north of Vaduz, the capital of Liechtenstein. Luis Fermán immigrated to Mexico, and after staying for

Miguel Fermán, Pancho Villa's half brother. Miguel was the legitimate son of Luis Fermán.
Courtesy of Center for Big Bend Studies, *The Secret Family of Pancho Villa: An Oral History*, by Rubén Osorio, published 2000

some time in Tamalipas, bought land, and settled near San Juan del Rio, Durango.

After the death of his wife, Rosario Gracia, Don Luis Fermán had a personal relationship with Micaela Arámbula, a maid in his home. As a result of that relationship, an illegitimate son was born. (1) When Osorio asked Dr. Fermán why the family relationship was never made public, the doctor said his grandparents and family always kept it a secret because it wasn't something the Fermáns were proud of. Being the product of an illicit relationship between Don Luis Fermán and a maid, the child's birth was considered shameful, not to be mentioned.(2)(3)

According to Dr. Fermán, while growing up the Arango boy worked as a *peon* on Luis Fermán's land. After Don Luis died, he continued to work for Luis Fermán's son, Miguel. With the passage of time, Doroteo Arango and his family moved to a ranch belonging to the López Negrete family.

Church records at San Juan del Rio show that on June 5, 1878, a child was born in Rio Grande, Durango, to Augustín Arango and Micaela Arámbula. He was baptized in the Church of San Francisco de Asís as José Doroteo Arango.(4)

In that same church, Augustín Arango and Micaela Arámbula baptized their four other children, Maria Ana, José Antonio, Maria Martina, and José Hipolito.

Further investigation led Osorio to the conclusion that Augustín Arango's relationship with José Doroteo Arango was that of stepfather, rather than that of a natural parent.

In the archives of the Church of San Francisco de Asís in San Juan del Rio, Durango, Osorio found documents verifying that at the end of the 1870s, the Arámbula-Alvarez family lived at the Cienega de Basoco. Micaela Arámbula was a member of this family.

Oral testimonies taken by Osorio during his search supported the probability that Micaela Arámbula was a maid at Cienega del Basoco. During the 1870s, Luis Fermán and Micaela Arámbula

vhere they had a master-maid relation-
y had an affair which produced an il-

information he had been able to obtain
cipal, parochial, and private archives,
the oral histories obtained from 28
ın Quiñonez, Fermán, and Quiñonez
rmation led Osorio to conclude that
1830s, an Austrian immigrant named
ıgin, a native of Liechtenstein, arrived
San Juan del Rio, Durango, where he
n as Cienega de Basoco. He married
parented a son, Luis.
on of Luis Fermán and Ursula Gurrola,
ⁱio. He spent his entire life at Cienega
de Basoco. He married Rosario Gracia, and they had two sons,
Luis in 1869 and Miguel in 1870. Both were born at Cienega
de Basoco and baptized in the Church of San Francisco de Asís.

Based on his findings, Osorio concluded that José Doroteo
Arango, known as Francisco "Pancho" Villa, was the illegitimate
son of Don Luis Fermán and Micaela Arámbula, but was listed
in his registered birth certificate as the son of Augustín Arango
and Micaela Arámbula.

Growing up, Villa developed charismatic charm. He was able
to attract and lead men. As a leader he achieved popularity and
success by giving to poor peons land and money which he seized
from the rich.

What kind of man was Pancho Villa? The family of F. Reid
Buckley and his brother, William F. Buckley, Jr., the archconserva-
tive journalist, had been engaged in business and lived in Mexico
for many years. William Buckley's father personally knew Villa.
He described Villa as a "homicidal maniac, as well as a patriot;
Villa was a bandit, a cold blooded murderer, and partly mad . . .
one of the most fascinating characters in Mexican history."(5)

Buckley said that in 1913 and 1914, Villa ruled his home state of Chihuahua like a medieval warlord. He financed his army by rustling herds of cattle, which he sold north of the border, where there was no shortage of people in the United States willing to sell him guns and ammunition. In Chihuahua, toward the end of 1913, he proclaimed himself governor, and issued his own currency, called *bilimbiques* by most Mexicans. If merchants refused to accept the bilimbiques,[3] they were shot.

A ruthless man, Villa would order an execution on a whim. Ordinarily, but not always, he left the actual killing to his friend, Rodolfo Fierro, a feared Villa executioner known as *El Carnicero* (The Butcher).(6)

Bilimbique printed by Villa's Chihuahua government in 1915

In spite of these sordid events, Villa maintained his popularity by breaking up vast holdings of the hacendados and parceling them out to the widows and orphans of his soldiers.(6)

Buckley continues: "He was bigger than life, by turns cruel and generous, vicious and magnanimous . . . a *zampatortas* (glutton, boor), a swaggering, mustachioed lover, who danced all night with female camp followers and, according to one of his last surviving widows, married twenty-six times. It was said that when Villa

---

3 Bilimbique–popular name given in Mexico to bank paper money printed during the Mexican revolutions by temporary governments of the various leaders of the Mexican revolutions. The money became worthless once the leader vacated the temporary office.

encountered a fair maiden that he wished to bed, but who insisted on marriage before cohabitation, he would tell one of his men to summon a priest to perform the marriage on the spot."

V. Blasco Ibaňez, in his book *Mexico in Revolution*, described Villa in 1920:

"Villa does not smoke. Villa does not drink. His only weakness is women, and the presence of a woman is enough to upset him completely. One might suppose such a man capable of carrying off a lady by main force. Worse things than that figure in Villa's biography. But, as a matter of fact, Villa is a man of principle. *Things have to be done proper like*, says he. *The way God and Holy Mother Church commands.*"

It was reported, says Ibaňez, that when he found a woman to his liking, Villa married her with all the established rights and greatest possible solemnity.

He once promoted an Indian curate, a relative of his, to be a bishop, to celebrate in suitable dignity, miter and all, his marriage to a Mexican stenographer. The employee in charge of the government marriage registry brought his book to the ceremony. Villa, who could write nothing but his name, signed the matrimonial record. Then he went off with his bride to his private Pullman car.

When Villa woke up the next morning, the first thing he did was send for the marriage license man and his book. The poor devil obeyed the summons, trembling like a leaf, sure his time had come.

"You have that book," Villa demanded. "Show me the page."

The record was pointed out to him, and the text explained. He was convinced when he recognized his own signature. Then he calmly tore out the leaf, folded it up, and put it in his pocket. At last his conscience was clear.

Ibaňez continues, with tongue in cheek: "He was a man of morals, with respect for established institutions. He was faithful to his first wife, his real wife, and he intended to remain so. He was not going to leave any documents around that someday might cause a scandal."

Gen. S.L.A. Marshall, in an oral account given to the Institute of Oral History in El Paso, spoke of an incident that reportedly happened in a bar and gambling joint in Juarez called El Gato Negro (the Black Cat).

Villa poses with unknown "bride".
Courtesy of Center for Big Bend Studies, *The Secret Family of Pancho Villa: An Oral History*, by Rubén Osorio, published 2000

One evening at the Gato Negro, Villa was enjoying an expansive mood, and pointed to a high Spanish comb worn by a dance hall girl. He bet Rodolfo Fierro, one of his generals, that he could shoot the comb off the girl's head without hitting her. Fierro bet him twenty-five dollars he couldn't. Villa pulled out his big Colt .45, aimed, and fired. The girl, shot through the head, fell dead. Villa, with a sheepish smile, counted out twenty-five dollars and handed them over to Fierro. It was considered quite a joke.(7)

A large part of Villa's success could be attributed to three of his generals who were ardent followers. The first, Felipe Angeles, graduated from the Mexican military academy at Chapultepec and the French military academy in St. Cyr, France. He was considered one of the best artillery commanders in the entire Mexican revolution. Because of injuries, he was unable to discharge his military duties, so Villa sent him in 1915 as his representative to Washington, D.C., hoping that Angeles could induce the U.S. government to become more supportive of his quest for power in Mexico.

Rodolfo Fierro (The Butcher) at machine gun.
Courtesy of El Paso Public Library, Aultman Collection

Two other close personal friends and strong followers were Rodolfo Fierro (The Butcher) and Tomás Urbina, both capable generals who helped Villa win many military battles.

Urbina was murdered by Fierro for "betraying his friend, Pancho." Just a month after the murder, Fierro died when he drowned in quicksand while en route with Villa's army to Agua Prieta in October of 1915.

Even without the guidance and assistance of these three generals, Villa pursued his goal of seizing Sonora (Agua Prieta, Naco, and Hermosillo—all lost battles). He continued his raids in northern Mexico and, famously, in Columbus, New Mexico, until friends secured a grant of amnesty from the Mexican government. In return, he would agree never to fight the government again.

Tired, and aware that he could never climb to his former political and military heights, he accepted the terms of surrender. The Mexican government gave him the 25,000-acre Canutillo Ranch in Chihuahua. In addition, he received generous funds for farm equipment, building materials, and tools, as well as pensions for his men. Included in the package was a provision for a personal armed guard of fifty of his *dorados* (his "golden ones"), with pay.

The bandit—now country squire—built roads, farmed, and educated dozens of children. It seemed that Villa had found peace at least.

He was the only foreign military personage ever to invade the continental United States and get away with it. In the northern regions of Mexico, his name is at times uttered with respect, and in the United States, it has been kept alive by Hollywood and pulp fiction.

One thing for sure, the name Pancho Villa is well known.

3

"THOSE FELLOWS WE SHOT"

Living and ranching in Mexico, particularly Sonora and Chihuahua, during revolutionary days was dangerous and challenging.

The Mexican revolutions, which began in 1910 and continued until 1929, caused great chaos and bloodshed. Groups of bandits marauded and preyed upon helpless people in great numbers. Young boys and men joined rebel armies, as well as federal government forces, in order to provide a way of living and work. Many were pressed into service by not only the federal government, but also by revolutionaries. When military service was demanded of a man or boy, if he refused, the alternative was to be taken out and shot by firing squad, or hanged.

One of Pancho Villa's trusted subordinates was Gen. Rodolfo Fierro. The Mexican people called him *El Carnicero* (The Butcher). A story circulated that El Carnicero at one time lined up prisoners four deep for execution. He would then shoot through all four with a single bullet, and proclaim proudly how he saved bullets.

Dad (Ben F. Williams, Sr.) was born in Mexico in 1901. He spent time as a young boy in Beloit, Kansas, attending school to

Triple execution in Mexico.
Courtesy of Arizona Historical Society

Execution of 256 of Villa's enemies.
Courtesy of Arizona Historical Society

learn English, after which he returned to the Santa Rosa Ranch, located ten miles northwest of Nacozari, where he worked for Granddad (Marion Williams). For those who were ranching and living in Mexico, it was a rough and perilous life.(1)

4-cylinder Dodge in front of Granddad's Santa Rosa Ranch

When Dad was sixteen years old, Granddad took him to the hardware store in Douglas and bought him a .45 Colt six-shooter. He then had a cartridge belt cut down to Dad's size and a holster made at the local saddle shop for the pistol. Dad carried the pistol when he was cowboying on the Santa Rosa. Granddad carried a Colt six-shooter as well.

The perils of revolutionary days can best be illustrated by a story told to me by Granddad. The Santa Rosa had been visited by bandits who claimed to be revolutionaries; they appropriated most of his better cowponies. What

Ben F. Williams, Sr., at age 16, taken in Douglas

29

mounts he had left after the thievery were kept in the horse pasture about a mile and a half from ranch headquarters.

Granddad had moved his family to Douglas in 1911 because of the revolution and dangers of the times.(2) He'd hired Bob Hiler as foreman to run the ranch. Hiler was born in Friotown, Texas, in 1877, and lived most of his years on the Mexican border.

Bob was a completely bilingual gringo who knew well the customs and ways of the Mexican people. He was soft spoken, but meant what he said. Those who knew him realized he was not a person to trifle with. The *vaqueros* (cowboys) on the ranch liked and respected him.

It was fall roundup time in 1912, and Hiler had hired extra men to gather the cattle to ship to Douglas.[4] The horses needed for the roundup, which was to commence on the following day, were lazily resting in the shade of a large mesquite tree in the front yard next to the house. Five cowboys, in addition to Hiler, were gathered after lunch in the shade of the same big tree, talking, passing the time of day, and enjoying a smoke in the cool autumn breeze.

Juan Pedro, one of the cowboys, commented, "Roberto, I see five men riding this way down the road. They're about a kilometer away."

Hiler remarked, "You're right, Juan Pedro. I'm going to get the glasses so I can get a better look." He entered the house and returned with his binoculars. After a good look at the riders through the glasses, he commented to the cowboys, "I don't recognize any of those fellows, but I can tell you that the horses they're riding are plumb worn down. Some of those men are armed. I don't know what they're up to, but I'll bet it's no good. What with all the revolutionaries and bandits around, they could mean trouble. You boys take your rifles and go inside, stand by the windows,

---

4 They had been sold to Harold Tovrea, a good friend of Granddad's and, at times, partner in various cattle deals. Tovrea owned the Tovrea Feeding and Meat Packing Company in Phoenix, where he built a unique and ornate home in southeast Phoenix, which the locals referred to as the "Tovrea castle." It still stands today, and remains a notable Phoenix landmark.

and watch me. If I have any trouble, I'll touch the brim of my hat with my hand. If I do that, you open fire and shoot to kill."

The vaqueros disbursed, went into the house with their .30-.30 carbines, and stood behind the windows. They could see out but couldn't be seen from outside the building.

It wasn't long before the strangers rode up and dismounted. As they approached, Hiler greeted them in Spanish, saying, *"Hóla! Que están haciendo por aqui?"* (Hello, what are you doing here?)

The leader answered, *"Estamos pasando por aqui y nuestros caballos estan cansados.* (We're passing through here and our horses are tired.) *Necitamos caballos frescos para continuar.* (We need fresh ones to continue.)"

Hiler said, "I'm sorry, boys, but we don't have any fresh horses. Some of Carranza's men came last week and took all but those you see here. We're starting our roundup tomorrow morning and need these horses."

Without hesitating, the group's leader said, "You don't need those horses as bad as we do, so we're just gonna take 'em."

Hiler said, "Don't do that, boys. Go find some horses somewhere else. We need these."

The leader shouted an order to his men, "Go get their horses."

Hiler reached to his hat and touched the brim. Instantaneously there echoed thundering reports from five saddle guns. The strangers fell dead in their tracks.

Bob's men came quickly out of the house, and Hiler said, "Boys, this is very serious business. We've got to dispose of these bodies and horses. Put the bodies over the saddles, and we'll lead the horses over to the limestone cliffs up north. And don't ever mention this to anyone because it could cause serious problems."

They agreed that no one would say a word about the killings. Then they loaded the bodies over the saddles of the worn-out horses and led them two miles from the ranch house to some steep cliffs. Over the centuries, erosion had created deep crevices in the limestone bluffs.

The vaqueros took the horses bearing the bodies to the edge of a cliff. There, they shot the horses and pushed them with the bodies over into the crevices where they couldn't be seen.

Not a word was said, and the following day the roundup began. It took ten days to finish, after which Hiler went to Douglas to visit his family. He saw Granddad in Douglas, but said nothing about killing the intruders at the Santa Rosa.

After staying a couple of days in Douglas, Hiler returned to the ranch. Not long thereafter, Granddad went from Douglas back to the ranch. He had advised his foreman that he would be down on a particular day, so the foreman had a cowboy saddle Granddad's horse to take to meet him. In those days, people traveling from Agua Prieta to Nacozari could ride the train, which could be flagged down and stopped at a point not far from the Santa Rosa. When the train stopped, Juan Pedro was waiting with Granddad's horse "Fox," saddled and ready to go to ranch headquarters not far away.

As they rode, they crossed over the Barregon mountains. Near the top, under a hackberry tree, was a spring of cool water. It was a favorite place to stop, water your horse, have a drink, and rest for a while before continuing your journey.

As they were resting after a good drink of water, Juan Pedro said to Granddad, "You know, Don Mariano, we never heard anything about those fellows we shot."

Not knowing what he was talking about, but realizing that there was something that he wanted to know, Granddad egged Juan Pedro on until he had been told all about the incident.

On arrival at the ranch, Granddad was greeted by Bob Hiler, and shortly thereafter they had their evening meal. After dinner, the two were seated on the porch in the cool of the evening when Granddad said to Hiler, "Bob, tell me about those strangers who were shot and killed."

Hiler said, "Marion, how in the world did you hear anything about that? We swore we wouldn't say a word to anybody."

Granddad said, "Well, I just happened to find out, and I want to know about it."

Hiler told him the entire story. Nothing further was ever mentioned about the shootings or disposition of the strangers' bodies and horses.

Living and ranching in Mexico during revolutionary days was tough.

Granddad, Marion L. Williams, at the Slaughter Ranch

4

GRANDDAD AND THE GENERAL

My grandfather, Marion L. Williams, had been a cattle rancher in northern Sonora for a number of years before the Mexican revolutions began. During the revolutions, Granddad was a co-owner of the Santa Rosa Ranch (ten miles northwest of Nacozari, Sonora), where he raised cattle and a family. My grandfather and another American, Frank Bishop, a lawyer living in California, formed a partnership and together owned the enterprise. It was Granddad's job to operate the ranch and care for the cattle.

Frank came to the ranch once a year to look things over and spend time with Granddad. They were not only business associates; they were also good friends.

In 1911, with the Mexican revolution well underway and Pancho Villa on the rampage, Granddad sent his family to Douglas. There, he maintained a family home and continued to own and operate the Santa Rosa, which carried several thousand head of steers. The revolution was in full swing when Granddad drove 1,000 head north from the Santa Rosa and crossed them at the Agua Prieta port of entry.

In those days, there was a duty of $10 per head imposed by the Mexican government on the exportation of Mexican cattle. Granddad paid $10,000 at the Mexican customs house in Agua Prieta, and gave it no further thought until a short time later when he had a phone call. J.S. Williams, manager of the Moctezuma Copper Company, was a good friend. He said he wanted to talk to Granddad.

Granddad went to Williams' office in Douglas, where he was told that Gen. José Maria Maytorena had issued a warrant for the arrest and execution of Marion Williams. The order to his troops specified that should Marion be caught within Maytorena's lines, he was to be hanged.

The warrant came to J.S. Williams' attention in a telegram addressed to him by mistake. He knew the warrant was not meant for him, but rather for his friend, Marion.

When Granddad and Williams met at the Douglas office, J.S. cautioned, "I wanted to tell you about the warrant, Marion, so you'll know to stay out of there."

Maytorena's headquarters was in Naco, Sonora, where the general had set up a command post in a Pullman car parked on a railway siding.

Granddad had paid his $10,000 export duty to General Alvaro Obregón, military commander at Agua Prieta. The two opposing military forces, one in Naco and the other in Agua Prieta, had established a division line between them at Anavacachi Creek, a place midway between the two armies.

Although he was only 5'7" tall, my Granddad, a wiry little *gringo*, had enough spunk for half a dozen *hombres*. Upon learning of the warrant, he got in his automobile and drove directly to Maytorena's headquarters in Naco. The door to the general's office was guarded by two soldiers armed with Mauser army rifles. Williams greeted them in Spanish, asking to be permitted to pass. Permission was granted.

When Granddad knocked on the door to the general's office,

it was opened by Epigmenio Ybarra, who had at one time been cashier of the Bank of Cananea. Granddad and Ybarra had known each other well for a long time and were friends.

Ybarra cheerfully greeted Granddad, "Don Mariano. I'm very glad to see you. Come in. The general is here."

Granddad entered the office, and Ybarra introduced the two men.

The general declared, "Mariano Williams, don't you know I've given an order to my troops that you be hanged if you're caught inside my lines?"

"Yes," Granddad replied. "That's what I came over to see you about. Why did you issue such an order? What have I done?"

"You exported 1,000 head of steers through Agua Prieta and paid General Obregón $10 a head export duty. That shows your partisanship."

"That doesn't show anything," said Granddad. "I'm an American trying to operate under revolutionary conditions. As far as I'm concerned, I'll pay whoever's in control at Agua Prieta. I don't give a damn who it is. I'm just trying to protect my own. I'll pay you if you want me to. All you have to do is take command of Agua Prieta."

The two men continued to talk. Granddad said that the general walked up and down the car several times and finally said, "You have a point. I can appreciate your position. You are right!"

He turned to Ybarra and said, "Write out an order saying that any time Don Mariano comes inside my lines . . . he's to be supplied with 50 armed men as escorts, if he wants them, to insure his safe passage while in our territory."

Ybarra wrote the order and handed it to Maytorena for his signature, saying, "General, you owe me a case of champagne."

"Why, what do you mean?"

"Don't you remember? When you told me to write the order that Marion Williams was to be hanged if he was found inside our lines, I told you that as soon as he found out about it, he'd be over here to see you. You said, 'You couldn't get that gringo here under any condition.' We bet a case of champagne on it."

"That's right, by God," Maytorena replied. "I owe you a case of champagne."

Marion L. Williams

5

THE KETTLE OF REVOLUTION:
THE CANANEA RIOTS

Many historians feel the spark that ignited the Mexican revolutions was the labor riots that took place in June 1906 at Cananea, Sonora.

Although the workers for Col. William C. Greene and his Cananea mining enterprise were the highest paid in the Mexican republic, union organizers and other agitators instilled discontent and anger among the copper company's workers. Feelings were running high; workers were mad.

True, Mexican miners were not paid the same as American workers. Further, foremen in the workforce were all Anglo. The miners wanted fewer hours and more pay: an increase from three pesos to five pesos. These inequities laid a good groundwork for agitators wanting to build a case against the mines.

Trouble broke out on Friday, June 1, 1906, when a large group of striking Mexican laborers marched to the lumber company which was managed by two American brothers named Metcalf. The Metcalfs ordered them to disburse. They refused, and the strikers surged forward. In an attempt to repel the strikers, one of the brothers turned on a high-pressure fire hose and doused the group with a forceful blast of water.

Instead of dispursing, the strikers became violent and set the lumber yard on fire. In the melee that ensued, the two brothers were killed, stabbed many times by miners' iron candlesticks (pointed, dagger-like candle holders for use in the mines). Three strikers also died at the scene of the fire.

Tom Rynning, Captain of the Arizona Rangers, led a group of Bisbee Volunteers, although he had been ordered by the Arizona governor not to cross over into Mexico. He resigned his commission and stepped over the line with the other volunteers, all of whom were immediately sworn into the Mexican Army before proceeding by train to Cananea.

Striking workers in Cananea confront U.S. soldiers protecting the company store, June 1906. Unknown photographer

Reinforcements from Bisbee answered Col. Greene's call for help and sped to Cananea with weapons. Mexican federal troops were ordered to proceed to Cananea as well. Col. Emilio Kosterlitzky, commander of the Mexican state police, was also summoned to Cananea from Magdalena, Sonora. He arrived with seventy-five *rurales* (Mexican rural state police) and immediately proceeded to round up the agitators, whom he hanged the following day. A total of 125 to 135 men, American and Mexican, were killed during the melee.

The entire story of the riots at Cananea is fascinating from a historical perspective. Granddad was present during the turmoil and wrote to his sister, Frances Holbrook, in Kansas about the incident. In his letter he reported:

Group of Kosterlitzky's rurales standing around dead revolutionaries in a cemetery. Note crosses and headstones.
Courtesy of El Paso Public Library, Aultman Collection

"Bacoachi, Sonora, Mexico   July 28, 1906

"I supose you have heard of the Cananea trouble I was their their was about thirty five men killed in all Six or Seven americans and the balance mexicans it looked like was dilbaret I did not take any part in the trouble as I have every thing in this country and I could not aford to take part in the fight and now everything is quiet and no more trouble and I do not think their will be as there is five hundred Soldgers Stationed at Cananea to keep down trouble... (signed) your Brother, Marion Williams"

This brief event gives a flavor of the hard, tough times that existed in northern Mexico. Feelings of revolution came about because of the enforcement of central power by Porfirio Diaz, who served as dictatorial ruler of Mexico for thirty years. Under the Diaz government, a select few prospered and led lives of privilege, while the vast masses of peons, for the most part, lived in poverty and serfdom.

The kettle of revolution began to boil, and later erupted into serious hostilities and fighting, which lasted from 1910 to 1929 in the Mexican republic. Death and destruction were experienced throughout the republic, and particularly in the northern states of Chihuahua and Sonora. At the same time, the popular revolutionary leader Emiliano Zapata and his large army of followers were creating havoc in the southern part of the country.

In 1914, Zapata and Pancho Villa, both at the zenith of their power, were to briefly share the presidential chair in Mexico City.

Left to right: Tomas Urbina, Pancho Villa (in presidential chair), Emiliano Zapata, Otilio Montaño.
Courtesy of C.L. Sonnichsen Special Collections Department, The University of Texas at El Paso, El Paso photo file PH001

6

PANCHO VILLA'S DORADOS
AND OTHER FIGHTING MEN

Pancho Villa's *dorados* ("golden ones") were organized in Ascensión, Chihuahua, in 1913. They were early-day commandos, men chosen carefully for their iron nerve and courage.

Freiderich Katz, a Villa biographer, wrote that the dorados were important to Villa. At first, they served only as his bodyguard, but they soon became an elite unit used for various purposes ranging from adjutants to executioners. And, like Napoleon's old guard, they were sent into battle when the odds were desperate.

When the dorados were created after the battle of Torreón in 1913, they consisted of three units of 100 men each. Villa chose all of his golden ones personally, on the basis of their loyalty to him and their prowess in battle. The dorados included many of his relatives, since he felt he could count on their unconditional loyalty (which was not always the case).

Whenever Villa heard about a soldier or an officer who had distinguished himself by a particular act of bravery or of resourcefulness, he recruited him into the dorados. For example, Candelario Cervantes attracted Villa's attention when during an attack on

Villa's dorados   (Villa-front row-here. ^)
Courtesy of Dutch and Cherie Salmon, High-Lonesome Books, Silver City,
New Mexico

the hacienda of Santa Clara, in which the Villistas had no artillery support, Cervantes loaded a few pieces of wood on a mule train, approached the enemy lines, and loudly gave orders for his soldiers to prepare an artillery attack on the hacienda. The federal soldiers, fearing an artillery barrage, panicked and surrendered.

Carlos Gutierrez Galindo's experience also captured Villa's attention and led to his incorporation into the dorados. He had been wounded and his horse killed during an unsuccessful attack. After his unit retreated, federal soldiers swarmed over the battlefield, killing all the wounded and prisoners. Gutierrez Galindo gutted his dead horse and hid for hours under its skin until Villista troops advanced once again and he was able to emerge from his hiding place.

Most dorados were of peonage ancestry, born and raised on farms and ranches. There were also villagers, family men, and common everyday folks as well. Why these men were called dorados is still a matter of controversy. Some believe that it was because they wore golden insignia on their hats. Others claim it arose from

the gold coins with which they were paid. Others saw an analogy to a famous nineteenth century group of Mexican bandits called *Los Plateados* (The Silver Ones).

Villa's dorados knew how to live off the land when necessary. They were superb horsemen, as was Villa. One can compare them perhaps to the horsemen of Genghis Khan of centuries ago.

Each dorado owned two horses and was equipped with a 7-millimeter carbine, a brace of .44-caliber Colt pistols, and 300 rounds of ammunition.

A game at which they were expert and skilled was usually played in a dry sand wash. One of the dorados would bury a live chicken in the sand so that only its head and neck were above ground. The object of the competition was for a mounted horseman to bend from his saddle and pluck the chicken out of the sand while riding at full gallop. Few competitors could best a seasoned dorado in a game of "chicken plucking."

Whenever a quick victory was needed, Villa sent in his golden ones. If his ragtag peon soldiers began retreating, the dorados were put into the fray to turn the tide of battle.

They were his shock troops, his pride and joy. He knew all of them by name. He purchased each man a 5X Stetson and olive drab uniform. They drilled until they pranced with the precision of the White Horse Guard.[5]

During one of his meetings with Gen. Hugh L. Scott in Juarez, Villa insisted that the American general witness his dorados perform on the parade grounds. After the golden ones had galloped past in rigid formation, Villa said, "How do you like them, General?"

Said Gen. Scott, "As a cavalry unit, General Villa, I assure you that I consider it the first in America."[6]

But it couldn't last. In June of 1914, Pancho and his bodyguard of dorados led dashing cavalry charges that overwhelmed Saltillo, then Zacatecas, in fiercely fought battles. As time passed, Villa and Carranza became bitter enemies. Later, Alvaro Obregón, one of Carranza's generals, taunted Villa into attacking his positions at Celaya. Counseled by Germans fresh from trench warfare in Europe, the Sonoran general arranged a nasty trap composed of zigzag trenches laid out behind immense spans of barbed wire. This horse-killing contrivance was completely covered by interlocking machine guns, set up and sandbagged to cover every entrance into the small city.

Obregón's cavalry was held in reserve, but it wasn't needed. In his dashing, hell-bent-for-leather style, Villa led a saber-rattling charge straight into the fortifications. Horses screamed and fell into the entangling wire, their defiant riders leaping up only to be shot down by French Maxim machine guns. Hundreds died. Bloodied, Pancho and his troops fled for cover.

Unable to believe that the nineteenth-century tactics which had served him so well could fail, Villa hit the Celaya defenses again. It was another slaughter. The Villista cavalry was wiped out, including the ragged remnants of his once-proud dorados. Villa's

5 The White Horse Guard was a British horse-mounted unit of highly trained troopers. They were used as a guard for the British royal family and on ceremonial occasions. They wore distinctly colorful uniforms with red tunics and white plumes in their hats. There were sometimes mounted on white horses.
6 *Pancho Villa, Strong Man of the Revolution*, by Larry A. Harris.

infantry dropped their rifles and ran.

Edwin Emerson, a newspaperman and a secret agent of U.S. Chief of Staff Leonard Wood, was greatly impressed by Villa's *Division del Norte*. He spent several months witnessing its greatest battles. He called the men of the Division del Norte "the best set up, best armed, best mounted, best equipped, best clothed, best fed, best paid and generally best cared for troops I have yet seen in Mexico."

When Villa was at his zenith, he succeeded in gaining widespread support in the United States, ranging from the Wilson administration to large American business interests, and the American political left favored him as well. What the Wilson administration and the business interests admired was the discipline Villa was able to keep when his troops occupied a city. All bars were closed, and any soldier caught looting was immediately executed. Many expressed great praise of General Villa.

Train carrying Villa's troops and their families. Note makeshift tent on top of boxcar.
Unknown photographer

After the capture of the city of Torreón, the United States consul reported to his superiors, praising Villa for being an able leader who could maintain order.

American support was enhanced by the fact that in order not to lose access to American arms and supplies, Villa refused to confiscate or touch American properties in any way. For leftists in the United States, Villa, because of his massive redistribution of goods, became the personification of social revolution in Mexico.

Villa was unable to achieve, however, any sort of permanent agreement with the other major revolutionary faction that had revolted in the north and which was headed by the governor of the state of Coahuila, Venustiano Carranza. What separated the two men was far more than their differing social origins, though they were great. (Villa had been a *peon* on a *hacienda*, while Carranza, a *hacendado* (landowner), had held important positions in the Diaz administration.) Their political and social views were incompatible.

And at the end of 1915, after Villa's disastrous Sonoran campaign, there was a widespread consensus among American observers, Carranzista leadership, and most of Villa's generals that the former head of the Division del Norte was finished in military terms. Some U.S. officials believed that Villa would seek asylum in the United States. By this time, Villa's command, comprised of those few who were roaming through Chihuahua, was so insignificant that Governor Enriquez of Chihuahua asked Carranza for only 2,000 men to contain the Villistas.

Towards the end of his fighting career, at a meeting held in 1920 at the Hacienda de Bustillos, Villa tried to rally support for an attack against the United States at El Paso. Whatever hopes he might have had to rally his army to his cause were quickly diminished when 23 of his 27 generals clearly stated that they did not wish to continue with the civil war, but rather wanted to accept Carranza's offer of amnesty.

An agreement was reached between Villa's dissenting generals and representatives of Obregón and Carranza to surrender the bulk of the Division del Norte. Obregon agreed to grant amnesty to all of Villa's soldiers and officers, with the exception of five men, which included Villa and his brother, Hipolito. Each Villista soldier would receive mustering-out pay, to which Obregon added ten dollars in gold, and they would have the choice of either joining Carranza's army or going home. Forty generals, 5,046 officers, and 11,128 soldiers laid down their arms.

In the meantime, Villa, with only a few hundred men, most of whom were dorados, faded away into the mountains. He had been offered an opportunity to leave Mexico, but elected to stay and fight.

Within a few months, more than 10,000 Americans (Pershing's forces) and several thousand Carranzista soldiers would roam unsuccessfully through Chihuahua trying to capture Villa. By the end of 1916, Villa again controlled a substantial portion of the state. His dissolving of the Division del Norte in no way signified that he was ready to give up fighting and to accept defeat. What he realized was that maintaining a regular army and waging regular warfare had become impossible for him. His men were demoralized, and he had neither the money nor the means to acquire arms and ammunition from north of the border to sustain an army.

About this time he decided to switch to guerrilla warfare, for which he needed only a small number of men. He was confident that if he should ever need his former soldiers again, he would be able to enlist them, either voluntarily or involuntarily, even though they had accepted amnesty from Carranza.

What Villa hoped for after his defeat in the Sonoran campaign was that most of his generals would again join him in the guerrilla war he was planning against both the Carranzistas and the Americans. His hopes were frustrated at the Bustillos conference, after which Villa retreated into the mountains of western Chihuahua.

His arrival there must have been one of the saddest days of his life. Only a few hundred followers, mainly the remnants of his elite guard of dorados, were left of an army that had once totaled 50,000 men. All trappings of regular warfare that had so strongly fascinated Villa, the troop trains, the sanitary trains (hospital), and

Villista troop train–animals inside, troops outside, Villa's dorados on left. Courtesy of Dutch and Cherie Salmon, High-Lonesome Books, Silver City, New Mexico

the artillery, were gone. Practically all of the generals had left him. After years of warfare that ended in defeat, his popularity among the civilian population of Chihuahua had reached an all-time low.

The possibility of securing arms in the United States was less than ever before, not only because of the U.S. arms embargo, but because the resources he had used in earlier years to pay for those arms, cattle from expropriated haciendas and the cotton of the laguna area, had been depleted. In spite of this situation, Villa never considered the possibility of giving up and going to the United States to accept the asylum that Woodrow Wilson had offered him.

Although Villa had only a few hundred men, he knew that these men, mostly dorados, were fanatically loyal to him. The same was true of the officers who now replaced former generals of the Division del Norte who had left him. These new officers tended to be young men, mainly dorados, who had risen from the ranks.

Although Villa relied heavily at times on his female soldaderas,[7] he never permitted any into the ranks of his esteemed dorados.

Freiderich Katz wrote that some of Villa's fanatic followers were committing atrocities against the civilian population. One was known for cutting off the ears of Carranzista prisoners, while another forced inhabitants of his own village into Villa's army against their will, to participate in Villa's attack on Columbus, New Mexico.

After the defeats suffered during the Sonoran campaign, and President Wilson's recognition of Carranza as Mexico's leader, many Mexican historians and American observers felt that Villa had become completely irrational, driven only by his blind hatred for Americans, who he felt had betrayed him and caused his defeat in his Sonoran campaign.

Freiderich Katz, writing about the later assassination of Villa, stated that "he was assassinated in July 1923 by orders of Obregón and Plutarco Elías Calles, the minister of the interior and Obregón's eventual successor as president. Both feared that Villa might take part in an uprising against them, but they also seemed to have been strongly influenced in this by American representatives.

"For many years, successive Mexican governments tried either to convert Villa into a nonperson or simply designate him as a bandit, but they did not succeed."

---

7   See Chapter 7.

Revolutionary soldaderas.
Courtesy of C.L. Sonnichsen Special Collections Department,
The University of Texas at El Paso

7

THE SOLDADERAS

Pancho Villa would never have achieved the success he enjoyed had it not been for his *soldaderas*. The term included women soldiers and camp followers as well. The word, *soldaderas*, is an Aragonese word derived from *soldada*, which means to hire a female servant. Soldadas were female servants. Later, "soldadera" covered not only female servants, but female warriors and fighters in the ranks of the combatants.

When Pancho Villa's soldiers traveled, they were accompanied by their women. Some were wives, some were mistresses, and some were followers. Among other things, they took care of and cooked for their men, bringing with them their children.

The women who served during the revolution were both young and middle-aged. Some volunteered to fight, while others followed their husbands or were abducted. Soldaderas participated in most phases of army day-to-day operations in the field. Far from being promiscuous or submissive, soldaderas often expressed fierce independence and deep resolve in service to their men. The problems shared by the soldaderas created a sisterhood with common bonds.

Women became soldaderas for a variety of reasons. Some were

wives of soldiers, following them without question. Some probably had no understanding of the reasons for which their husbands were fighting, while others were well aware of the goals and ideals of the revolutionary struggle.

The soldaderas carried not only their children, but also camping gear such as cooking utensils, bedding, food, and other necessities to provide for their men. It generally was the women who scrounged around over the terrain to find foods which they prepared for their men and children. V. Blasco Ibañez wrote in 1921 that the army could have scoured the lands seven times for food and yet the soldaderas, when looking an eighth time, usually found something to eat in order to sustain their fighting men and themselves.

Women of the revolution were referred to as sloppy workers, cooking ladies, captain's pet, soldaderas, gossips, Janes, cockroaches, blabbermouths, troublemakers, and sluts. Other names included baldies, orphans, brave women, and women of pleasure. Today, all can be classified as *Adelitas*, the name generally conferred on Villa's soldaderas.

Pancho Villa transported his troops by rail during most of his campaigns, and his soldaderas oftentimes rode on the roofs of the railcars as "support troops" for their husbands or consorts. Some soldaderas were nothing more than young girls who were raped and kidnapped not only by Villistas, but by federal soldiers, as well. With no alternatives, they were forced to accompany their men and provide them with camp and bed comforts.

One incident was reported where a federal officer tried to rape the sister of a fifteen-year-old girl. The victim grabbed the officer's gun and shot him before immediately killing herself. Having witnessed this horrible tragedy, the surviving sister fled to join her father in the Sierra Madres, vowing to become a soldier in order to kill *federales*. She disguised herself as a man and called herself "Angel." Angel achieved fame and a reputation as a fierce fighter of the revolution.

However, a great number of women who were dedicated to the cause of the revolution required no male consorts. One in particular, Petra Herrera, led a revolutionary battalion that defeated the federal army in Mexico City, for which she was promoted to the rank of lieutenant. She went so far as to change her identity in order to remain in active service, and every morning pretended to shave her beard. She explained it just started to grow in order

Soldaderas of the revolutions.
Courtesy of C.L. Sonnichsen Special Collections Department,
The University of Texas at El Paso

to convince the other soldiers that she was a man.

She gained a reputation as an excellent soldier until one day she declared, "I am a woman, and I will continue to carry out my duties as a soldier, using my real name." Stunned as they were, her male counterparts and officers permitted her to continue to fight. Along with 400 other women, she participated in the second battle of Torreón on May 30, 1914. One of her fellow Villistas later declared that it was Petra Herrera who took charge of Torreón after the battle was over.

Although Petra had never been formally recognized after the

second battle of Torreón, she nevertheless was motivated to form her own brigade, which quickly grew from 20 to 1,000 women. Her command permitted no man to spend the night in the women's camp. Nighttime guards were posted, and were told to shoot anyone who tried to get close to the sleeping female soldiers without satisfactorily responding to the challenge of "Who goes there?"

Petra requested recognition as a general officer and permission to form her own unit. Her request was denied and her army was dissolved, forcing her to end her career working as a waitress in a Juarez cantina.

Another interesting soldadera was Maria Quinteras de Merás. She enlisted in Villa's army in 1910. By 1913, she had fought in ten battles and received many decorations. In several attacks, some almost suicidal, she galloped her large horse at the head of attackers. Soldiers serving with her thought she was part witch and couldn't be killed. They harbored a superstitious yet credible belief that she never lost a battle. Her husband served as a captain in her military unit. Some historians claim that the soldaderas numbered between twenty and thirty percent of the armed groups.

Anthony Quinn, the well-known and popular movie actor who starred in such films as *Zorba the Greek*, *Viva Zapata*, and *Lust for Life* (for which he won Oscars), wrote in his autobiography that his mother had been a soldadera. Quinn was born in Chihuahua, Mexico, on April 21, 1915, during revolutionary days, but in 1918, the Quinn family moved to California, where Manuela Oaxaca Quinn worked for the railroad.

During revolutionary days in Mexico, women had few rights. Men governed in accordance with the Mexican Civil Code of 1884. The code granted single women almost equal rights with males, except that a single woman had to reside with her parents until the age of thirty. On the other hand, married women had no rights. They could not divorce, vote, enter into a contract, dispose of or administer their personal property, or decide about education for their children. Prohibited from tutoring anyone other than their husbands, married women could not become schoolteachers.

Soldaderas were *coronelas* (colonels), *Adelitas*, female soldiers, or camp followers. Women of the battlefields for the most part were strong-hearted, courageous, and loyal to their cause. Some were, as noted, actually officers in the revolutionary forces. Mainly, however, the soldaderas served the function of quartermaster, which is the branch of our army that procures and provides food, supplies, and other needed materials. Soldaderas were armed and

Women of the revolutions.
Unknown photographer

usually wore bandoliers of bullets as part of their "uniforms." Several wore pistols in holsters at their waists.

At the request of the *Chicago Daily Tribune*, V. Blasco Ibañez, a Spanish realist novelist, screenwriter, and film director, wrote a series of articles about the Mexican revolutions. He described how the Mexican army was made up of both men and women, how Villa's camp followers contributed to the care and morale of his men, and at times engaged in battle alongside their male counterparts.

Ibañez also wrote *Mexico in Revolution*. In the book, he says that the soldier refuses to go anywhere without his "old woman."

This epithet is a term of endearment. The "old woman" could have been only twenty years old. That's the way it was in the Mexican army.

To count the women, you counted the soldiers. Every man had a woman who followed the regiment everywhere, each carrying a basket laden with food and utensils. Often there were a number of barefoot children trotting along at her side, some of them naked. They would smile at their daddies but keep an eye out for the officer, a much-feared god, who was always shooing them away when they ran up to take their father by the hand.

Around the barracks, doorways and sidewalks were crowded with women, sitting elbow-to-elbow in correct military alignment. With their black shawls over light-colored dresses, to observers they looked like so many penguins lined up on the edge of a cliff. Each of these women had a basket at her feet in which she had brought her man's dinner. The soldadera was faithful beyond reproach to her man.

Neither passion nor beauty figured in these unions. The quality the Mexican soldier most valued in his old woman was her skill in finding something to eat. When a soldier fell, he willed his woman to some more fortunate comrade in arms, or she went on her own to another man. Since the Mexican army took men of all ages, fifteen-year-old boys could be seen living with soldaderas old enough to be their mothers or their grandmothers. And there were wrinkled old men with white stubble on their chins who got their meals from girls in their teens, whom they had inherited from soldiers killed in battle.

It was during actual fighting in the field that the soldaderas proved their powers of endurance and self-sacrifice. Many Mexican generals thought of abolishing the soldaderas, but in the end had to compromise and finally seek their support. What else could be done in an army destitute of a supply and sanitary corps? The sick and the wounded could not be abandoned to chance. The soldadera made up for more than one deficiency in the Mexican military system. Not only did she look after her soldier, but at times her attention was needed by the chief.

"Have you a bite to spare?" the captain asked one of his men during a halt. The officer, not provided as a rule with a soldadera, was much worse off than the private.

"No, Captain, but the Indian will be back soon and she'll surely have something," the soldier replied. ("Indian" was another pet name used by the soldiers when they tired of "old woman.")

When the troops were on the march, soldaderas usually formed the advance guard. They kept several miles ahead, so that when the men arrived the fires would be burning and the meal ready. Towns and villages were more afraid of the women than of the soldiers themselves. Soldaderas marched for whole days with a brat clinging to either hand, while another invisible one awaited its call into the world. She carried a pack of clothes and bedding on her head and sometimes, to top it off, a pet parrot.

With so much to carry and take care of, you would think that the woman had enough to do. It has been said that she passed over the countryside like a scourge, and along her path not a piece of fruit remained on the trees, not a turnip remained in a garden, not a coop had a chicken, nor a barnyard a pig. She swept everything before her and left the landscape parched and barren. It was as though a plague of locusts had settled on the countryside. Those women could pick up a good meal in sterile places where any ordinary human would starve. A village may have been sacked seven times in one week, but give her the chance for one more meal and she would turn out a regular Sunday dinner.

Ibañez continues:

The Mexican's indifference to death was not courage, really. Courage is that positive compulsion a man in commodious circumstances feels when, voluntarily and fearlessly, he goes out to meet self-sacrifice and danger. The Mexican had, rather, a mere contempt for life. It was fatalism–absence of fear, more exactly. Death, no matter how terrible its form, would not prove much worse than life as he was living it. That was the feeling.

A Mexican could be at one and the same time both sentimental and cruel. He would burst into tears at a sad story and then order out a firing squad for an execution; he was passionately devoted to home and family but never satisfied unless he was tramping over mountains and deserts in support of an insurrection. Tradition also figured large in the minds of country people, especially in Mexico.

8

"IF I HAVE TO DIE TOMORROW, I MIGHT AS WELL DIE NOW"

Mexican music has always intrigued me, and I continue to enjoy its flavor today. My favorites are Mexican *corridos* about people and events whose stories are written and put to music.

Pancho Villa's men sang about their women and exploits in their corridos. The lyrics were spontaneously composed and put to music. One might ask, *what is a corrido?* It's a narrative song or ballad whose characters, events, and themes are representative of the history of people and local communities, in a musical language understood by Mexicans of all classes.

Corridos are a folk art form somewhere between oral history and cultural myth. The songs tell stories about local events and local people. They reflect local perspectives, at times with embellishments for dramatic effect.

During the Mexican Revolutions, corridos reflected the heartbeat of the Mexican community. Typical corridos addressed such themes as the entry of a presidential candidate into Mexico City, labor strikes, fuel shortages, soldiers and heroes like Pancho Villa and Emiliano Zapata. *Soldaderas*, women who took part in the revolution as soldiers and camp followers, became popular subjects as well. One Villista corrido tells us that "Pancho Villa and his people have arrived." "People" refers to his followers: men, women, and children.

Corridos reached their high point during the revolutions and are still sung today. Such corridos as "La Cucaracha," "La Valentina," "La Adelita," and others, are familiar to many Latinos on both sides of the U.S.-Mexico border. They are also sung at funerals to commemorate a person's life.

Corridos tell stories of battles won, the women who went to war with their soldier lovers, to cook and care for them, such as La Valentina and La Adelita, or the philandering Juan Charrasqueado who was killed for fathering yet another child out of wedlock.

Revolutionary musicians, ca. 1911.
Courtesy of El Paso Public Library, Aultman Collection

Mexico is peopled by music lovers, and its inhabitants turn to poetry and song by instinct. The most respected men in any regiment were the ones who could play a guitar to accompany their songs in the evenings. A musician's comrades looked after him and vied with one another in doing him favors. They kept him away from the firing line, and their first thought as a battle began was to see that the guitar was kept safe.

Another curiosity: With the exception of a tune sung by Villa's men called "La Cucaracha" (The Cockroach), most of the songs of the revolution were named after women, "La Adelita" and "La Valentina," for instance. The song "La Valentina" is the "Marsellaise" of present-day Mexico. When you hear that song around a Mexican camp, look out! A revolution is about to break out. And yet its lines are not bloodthirsty at all. It is the lament of a wandering drunkard addressing himself to a girl named Valentina. The last stanza alone is sufficient to justify the immense popularity of the song:

Valentina, Valentina,
Rendido estoy a tus pies
Si me han de matar mañana,
Que me maten de una vez.

Valentina, Valentina,
I lie at your feet.
If they are going to kill me tomorrow,
They might as well kill me now.

The whole psychology of the Mexican people at that time, its fatalistic resignation, contempt for death, acceptance of the misery of living, its inability to buck up and rise, was worked into the last two lines of "La Valentina." That is why the song is still loved so much. It expressed a national philosophy: *If I have to die tomorrow, I might as well die now.*

One of the most popular corridos of Pancho's revolutionary days was "La Adelita. The song remains immensely well liked even today. If you visit a border cantina, the jukebox will likely be blaring out the words and music about the sargento's (sergeant's) girlfriend, Adelita.

This corrido has to do with Pancho Villa's army coming out of Chihuahua with 10,000 men, headed to do battle at Agua Prieta:

En lo alto de la abrupta serranía
acampado se encontraba un regimiento
y una joven que valiente los seguía
locamente enamorada del sargento.

In the heights of a steep mountainous range a regiment was encamped and a young woman bravely follows them madly in love with the sergeant.

Popular entre la tropa era Adelita
la mujer que el sargento idolatraba
y además de ser valiente era bonita
que hasta el mismo Coronel la respetaba.

Popular among the troop was Adelita the woman that the sergeant idolized and besides being brave she was pretty that even the Colonel respected her.

Y se oía, que decía, aquel que tanto la quería:
Y si Adelita se fuera con otro
la seguiría por tierra y por mar
si por mar en un buque de guerra
si por tierra en un tren militar.

And it was heard, that he, who loved her so much, said:
If Adelita would leave with another man I'd follow her by land and sea if by sea in a war ship if by land in a military train.

Y si Adelita quisiera ser mi novia
y si Adelita fuera mi mujer
le compraría un vestido de seda
para llevarla a bailar al cuartel.

If Adelita would like to be my girlfriend If Adelita would be my wife I'd buy her a silk dress to take her to the barrack's dance.

Pancho Villa's horse, Siete Leguas (Seven Leagues),[8] was so popular that a corrido was composed about the famous mount.

Pancho Villa riding his favorite horse, Siete Leguas.
Courtesy CafePress.com

GENERAL PANCHO VILLA

---

8 The horse was so named because he was capable of carrying his revolutionary rider a distance of 28 miles a day for days on end.

The familiar tune and lyrics can be heard throughout the Mexican republic today, played and sung by mariachis. The revolutionary song is particularly popular in the northern states of Chihuahua and Sonora.

Siete Leguas el caballo	Seven Leagues horse
que Villa más estimaba.	Villa highly prized.
Cuando oía silbar los trenes	When he heard the train whistle
se paraba y relinchaba.	stopped and snorted.
En la estación de Hirajuato	At the station Hirajuato
cantaban los horizontes,	horizons sing,
allí combatió formal	formal fought there
la Brigada Bracamonte.	Bracamonte Brigade.
Oye tú Francisco Villa	Hey, you Francisco Villa
que dice tu corazón.	What says your heart.
Ya no te acuerdas, valiente,	Don't you remember, brave,
cuando tomaste a Torreón,	when you took to Torreón
ya no te acuerdas valiente	Don't you remember, brave,
que atacaste a Paredón.	Paredón attacking.
Como a las tres de la tarde	As at three p.m.
silbó la locomotora.	the locomotive whistled.
¡Arriba Villa, muchachos,	Hail Villa, boys,
suban la ametralladora!	stake up the machine guns!
Adiós torres de Chihuahua,	Goodbye Chihuahua towers
adiós torres de Pantera.	Farewell, Pantera towers.
Ya vino Francisco Villa	Villa just arrived
a quitarles la frontera,	to take away the border
ya llegó Francisco Villa	Villa is here
a devolver las fronteras.	to return the borders.

"La Cucaracha" is a fascinating and catchy tune which became popular on both sides of the border. The lyrics of the famous revolutionary mazurka told of the "cockroach" that couldn't go any more because it lacked a smoke of marijuana. The number of stanzas which were composed by Villa's soldiers was almost endless. Villa's troops could and did compose new stanzas as they proceeded in their long marches or around the campfire in the evenings, when the singing of songs was popular.

One stanza said that from the whiskers of Carranza, the singer was going to make a hatband and place it on the big hat of the brave Pancho Villa.

"La Cucaracha" is probably the most popular of all Mexican folk songs:

La cucaracha, la cucaracha	The cockroach, the cockroach,
Ya no puede caminar	It just can't go any more
Porque no tiene, porque le falta,	Because it lacks, because it's missing
Marijuana que fumar.	Marijuana for a smoke.
Un panadero fué a misa	A baker went to mass.
N oencontrando que rezar.	Couldn't think of what to pray for.
Entonces le pidió a la Virgen pura	So he asked the saintly Virgin
Pa' marijuana que fumar.	Marijuana for a smoke.
Una mujer fué la causa	Yes, a woman was the cause
De mi perdición primera,	Of my very first undoing
Y también de la segunda,	And also my second
Y también de la tercera.	And also my third.
De las barbas de Carranza	From the whiskers of Carranza
Voy hacer una toquilla,	I am going to make a hatband,
Pa' ponerla en el sombrero	And I'll place it on the big hat
Del valiante Pancho Villa.	Of the brave Pancho Villa.

When I was a teenager, I spent a summer with my Aunt Ella and Uncle Morris Browder at Granddad's San Bernardino Ranch.

The place at one time belonged to John Slaughter. There were four or five ranch hands and cowboys living there at the time. At the end of the day after work, a hand-and-facewash, and then dinner, the "boys" would gather in the back yard. One had a guitar and was very good at playing Mexican cowboy music. I watched him carefully and learned how to strum enough chords to play a few tunes. One of my favorite tunes was "Quatro Milpas" (Four Fields). It was a melancholy song telling sadly about a deserted

Ranch house remodeled by Marion L. Williams, Slaughter Ranch, the old San Bernardino.
Courtesy of Jay Dusard

ranch. I learned the chords and words to that song, and after a time I picked up more chords and played more songs. Other favorites of mine were "Juan Charrasqueado" and "Valentin de la Sierra." The latter was about a revolutionary leader who was captured by federal troops and killed in the mountains (shot and hanged, the song relates).

With the passage of time, I learned more chords and more songs, enabling me to play along with the mariachis. I enjoyed singing and playing with them.

When I attended the University of Arizona, I joined the Sigma Nu fraternity, where I continued to learn songs such as "Streets of Laredo," "Red River Valley," "Strawberry Roan," and "I've Been Workin' on the Railroad." Being the only brother in the Sigma Nu house who could play the guitar, invariably I was called upon to perform when we entertained young ladies from sororities at exchange dinners.

I still enjoy hearing Mexican corridos and cowboy songs,

although I'm no longer able to fret or finger chords with enough dexterity to play well.

Like a Coca Cola, the flavor and desire for more lingers afterwards.

9

SIETE LEGUAS AND THE MARBLE STAIRCASE

Stories abound relating to Pancho Villa and his exploits. Tales of his popularity and horsemanship are often told around Douglas, Arizona.

This story involves Pancho Villa and the Gadsden Hotel. Since it was built, the Gadsden has been the business and social center of Douglas where people congregate. I opened my first law office at the Gadsden on October 13, 1956. Dad, although not a lawyer, rented space on the ground floor next to the lobby and remodeled it into a small but attractive office for the two of us. He purchased new furniture, and the resulting offices complemented the old hostelry, which at one time belonged to Dad and Bud Warner. Rent was only $60 per month, which of course sweetened the deal.

The original hotel, built in 1907, was completely destroyed by fire in 1928. The building was four stories high and constructed of wood and other combustible materials.

The hotel was rebuilt in 1929 of concrete and steel. When it reopened, it was a thing of beauty, sporting large Italian marble columns in its lobby, whose high ceiling shone brightly with 200

Gadsden Hotel burning, 1928.
Courtesy of Cochise County Historical Society

Gadsden Hotel as it looks today.
Courtesy of Cindy Hayostek

Marble staircase at the Gadsden Hotel–with chip in 7th step.
Courtesy of Cindy Hayostek

ounces of carefully applied gold leaf. As I write this story, gold is quoted on the commodity market at $1,210 per ounce. The ceiling's current value would be $242,000.00!

An impressive and beautiful marble staircase was installed in the new building, leading from the lobby to the mezzanine on the lobby's east side. At the top of the staircase, gracing the wall, is a 42-foot original Tiffany stained glass window, an exquisite work of art. The builder of the Gadsden didn't spare any cost in rebuilding the five-story hostelry.

There is a legend that Pancho Villa rode his horse up the marble staircase, and that his horse, Siete Leguas (Seven Leagues), chipped a piece of marble from its seventh step. Indeed, Robin Brekhus, one of the current owners of the hotel, will show you the exact spot and the chipped step.

I set out to determine the truth of the story.

An essay written by Silas Griffin in March, 2009, describes an official, and only, public visit by Pancho Villa to Douglas. Griffin relates that a special train carrying Generals Alvaro Obregón and Pancho Villa, together with an entourage of approximately 200 members, traveled first from Nogales to Tucson and thereafter to Douglas.

The train arrived at the depot in Douglas at 2:30 p.m. on Monday, August 31, 1914. On the train's arrival, the Ninth Cavalry (Buffalo Soldiers) band was playing. A crowd of about 2,000 people milled around the station waiting to greet the train. Reports of the arrival and news were reported in the *Douglas International* newspaper in their issues of September 1 and 2 of 1914. They related that "this was Pancho's first visit to Douglas."

It was reported that Obregón, Villa, and 20 officers went by auto from the depot to the home of Francisco S. Eliás, where they were served lunch[9].

Among greeting dignitaries was Francisco Eliás, a well-known and politically potent resident of Douglas. Douglas mayor Ellis was on hand, as well as Roberto V. Pesquiera and J.U. Orozco from Agua Prieta, all excited to receive the visiting military leaders. Late in the afternoon of August 31, the entire assemblage motored to Agua Prieta for a celebration and many speeches.

That evening, a banquet was hosted by the Douglas Chamber of Commerce at the Douglas Country Club, during which the Ninth Cavalry band again played music. After a scrumptious dinner, which was attended by my grandfather Marion L. Williams, the party proceeded by auto back to the train depot, where they boarded and left late that night. Granddad told me about attending the dinner, and how Villa ate with his fingers and spilled food all over his clothes.

The train had originally been scheduled to leave at midnight on Monday, August 31, but its departure was delayed waiting for the arrival of Col. Plutarco Elías Calles, who was traveling from

9 It was reported that Villa gave each U.S. soldier in the complement of guards posted to protect the train while in Douglas a $5 gold coin.

Cananea by way of Naco to Douglas. Col. Calles would later command the troops defending Agua Prieta and successfully defeat Pancho Villa in his attack on Agua Prieta on November 1, 1915.

The special train then departed for El Paso, Texas, after the only open and public visit by Pancho Villa to Douglas, Arizona.

There were numerous reports, however, that at other times Villa slipped into Douglas for private social events. Connie Paul Kazal told me that her grandfather, Alfred Paul, Sr., and grandmother, Mabel Swain Paul, entertained Villa several times at dinner in their home on the corner of Tenth Street and C Avenue, directly across the street from the Immaculate Conception Church. Connie's grandmother was the daughter of George Washington Swain, who served as Arizona territorial circuit judge in the 1870s in Tombstone.

Now, back to the story about Villa riding his horse up the marble stairs at the Gadsden Hotel.

Gadsden Hotel, burned, 1928
Courtesy of Cochise County Historical Society

Villa's ride would have been prior to the destructive fire at the Gadsden in 1928, sometime between his rise as a revolutionary leader in 1911 and his military defeat at Agua Prieta in November of 1915.

I asked Robin Brekhus, one of the current owners of the Gadsden Hotel, about the marble staircase, and she informed me that three items survived the 1928 fire: the elevators, the bronze statues in the lobby, and the marble staircase.

But an examination of the photograph showing the remains of the hotel after the fire makes it hard to believe that any marble stairs survived.

Silas Griffin wrote that Villa's visit in 1914 lasted roughly 12 hours. He stated, "It would be as easy to state that General Villa drove his German limousine up a grand hotel staircase as it would be to believe he rode his horse up those legendary marble steps."

The two newspapers of the day, the *Dispatch* and the *International*, reported that Villa's visit of August 31, 1914, was his first, and that he never returned to Douglas thereafter.

Therefore, we must assume that during that visit, Villa did not ride a horse up the steps. At all times, according to newspaper reports, Villa was surrounded by members of the public gawking to see the famous revolutionary leader. Had he ridden a horse up the marble steps, it most certainly would have been published in the newspapers of the day.

Villa's other visits, such as his occasional dinner visits to the Paul home, would suggest that those visits occurred at times and under circumstances which Villa did not care to make public.

Silas Griffin concluded that, "Since generals Obregón and Villa were mobbed and scrutinized nonstop by many hundreds of local residents in Douglas and Agua Prieta from their arrival at 2:30 p.m. on August 31 to the ending of the evening banquet, General Villa, the centaur of the north, would have had to miraculously slip away undetected to prance up and down marble stairs like a Rudolph the red-nosed reindeer.

"Virtually impossible for a man of Villa's socio-political stature to have done something that public in so little time with no documentation of record whatsoever of the event.

"It is strictly an urban legend and could be based on the actions of a lesser known member of the Obregón-Villa entourage vying for a place in the brief and limited confines of the spotlight of fame."

Now, I don't want to be one to debunk a popular legend, so I leave it up to you, the reader, to reach your own conclusion. Did Pancho Villa ride his horse up the marble stairs, and did the horse's hoof chip the seventh step?

10

THE BATTLE FOR AGUA PRIETA

For several years, Pancho Villa was friendly with the United States and the Americans who were engaged in business and resided in the Mexican republic.

In 1915, when Villa struck out from Chihuahua to conquer Sonora, his soldaderas came along as well. In previous campaigns, Villistas acquired their food from the countryside along the way, but in this campaign they had to carry all of it.

Villa realized the march to Agua Prieta would be more arduous than any his men had ever undertaken because of the size of his army and the scarcity of food and water in the desert he had to travel through. For that reason, he took two steps to alleviate the suffering as much as possible. First, he decreed that no women would accompany the troops. This marked the only occasion that soldaderas were not permitted to follow their men on a major campaign.

The Casas Grandes, Chihuahua, staging point was 52 leagues distant (approximately 200 miles) from Villa's objective, Agua Prieta.[10] The terrain traveled by Villa and his troops was hostile

---

10 The town, founded in the late 1800s, was home for a Mexican customs house which collected handsome amounts of import and export duties, which in those days was paid in gold coin. The customs monies would help buy arms and munitions, as well as supplies. They would also pay his troops.

and had to be crossed by foot and horseback.

Villa ordered all camp followers placed on trains bound for Torreón. The troops cursed him for this, but Pancho realized women comprised more bulk than benefit on this campaign and would stress his meager supplies to the breaking point. Then he commanded the force to march in small contingents. Smaller groups would not deplete any available food and water resources as readily as his combined army of more than 10,000 men.

The Villistas' morale fell to a low ebb when they were deprived of their soldaderas. The low morale and the fact that they faced reinforced and better-trained government troops, led to the revolutionaries' defeat at Agua Prieta. Other contributing factors will be explained later in this chapter.

Perhaps a little background on the territory the Villistas passed through is in order here. In 1915, there were 4,225 Mormon settlers in Mexico, Mormons who had come to northern Sonora and Chihuahua to settle in such places as the Colonias Morelos, Oaxaca, Casas Grandes, Dublan, Juarez, Dias, Pacheco, Garcia and Chuichupa. They had come in the late 1800s, mostly from Arizona and Utah. These and other Mormon enclaves had fared well at the hands of Villa. He was friendly toward them and extended a warm measure of assistance and cooperation whenever possible. He had, as well, been careful to protect American lives and property.

After Porfirio Diaz's government broke up on May 25, 1911, fear and disorder plagued the Mormon settlements, particularly in Chihuahua, which were dominated by Villa, Salazar, Lopez, Gomez, and other revolutionary leaders. There was little prejudice against the settlers and not much actual antagonism expressed toward them. However, the Mormons had acquired a wealth of horses, wagons, supplies, ammunition, and weapons, all of which the revolutionary forces required.

Because of the hardships caused by the revolutions, it soon became evident to Chihuahua's Mormon settlers that their only course of action was to flee to the United States, so on July 29, 1912, most of them hurriedly boarded a train headed for El Paso. They were loaded into boxcars and cattle cars, along with their personal property, and hauled from Colonia Dublan to the border. The "exodus," as they called it, was made up of 1,500 Mormon refugees who established a camp in El Paso upon their arrival.

One of the Mormon elders, A.W. Ivins, wrote at the time that as soon as the colonists were gone, a campaign of looting and destruction was commenced by revolutionaries and local Mexicans against the Mormon properties. Stores were broken into and looted of hundreds of thousands of dollars worth of merchandise. Private homes suffered in the same manner. Livestock was appropriated. Almost every available thing of value was carried away or destroyed. At Colonia Diaz, most residences and public buildings were burned.

Other Mormon settlers left Morelos and Oaxaca in August of 1912 following news that the rebel Salazar was marching into Sonora. On hearing that news, a large number of women and children were sent north in 60 wagons. The wagons carried 450 people, who entered the United States at Douglas, where the column received a cordial reception.

Thereafter, more left for the United States, leaving behind only 25 men in the colonies as guards. Several groups moving toward the north were captured by Mexicans and robbed. The colonies had been entirely abandoned for some time when a Mormon party from Douglas went to check on their vacant properties. On its return, a member of the scouts wrote that on arriving at the colonies, they found every house had been looted and everything of value taken from Colonia Morelos. Sewing machines and furniture were ruthlessly smashed and lying around as debris. House organs, which were to be found in nearly every Mormon home, were reduced to heaps of kindling wood. Carcasses of dead animals lay about the streets. Doors and windows were smashed, stores gutted and contents strewn everywhere. Here and there a

Mormon camp during exodus from Colonia Morelos, August 1912.
Courtesy of Arizona Historical Society

cash register or some other modern appliance showed evidence of prejudicial destructive ignorance.

Final abandonment of the Mormon colonies was made in May, 1914, when 92 people from the three Sonoran colonies arrived in the U.S. aboard twenty-one wagons. They had been notified by the American Secretary of State that U.S. protection would not be extended to them in Mexico. Most of their property was left behind, at the mercy of the Mexicans.

Many of these fleeing Americans settled in the United States, a good number of them in Douglas. I attended Douglas schools with children of the dispossessed Mormons.

When revolutionary hostilities broke out in Sonora, Granddad—although not a practicing Mormon—moved his family from the Santa Rosa Ranch to a home he owned on Seventh Street in Douglas. He wanted his family out of harm's way, and an American family was safer in Douglas than at the remote location of Granddad's Santa Rosa Ranch.[11] The ranch was approximately ten

11 Granddad started his family after he married Teresa del Rio at Bacoachi, Sonora, in 1896. The wedding was performed by civil authorities because the Catholic priest from Arispe, 75 miles away, who Granddad had approached to do the honors, wanted 500 pesos, a princely sum at that time. The priest probably set the stipend high because he knew he would be uniting a good Catholic woman and a fallen-away Mormon.

miles northwest of Nacozari,(1) and could be reached in those days only on foot, on horseback, or by wagon. He continued his ranching operations during the troubled times of the revolutions.

An article in the *Douglas Daily Dispatch* dated March 21, 1913, stated that rebel successes had given them control of much territory, to the embarrassment of Huerta's federal government, and helped finance the revolution. The rebels reopened the entry port of Agua Prieta on March 20, 1913, and their first day's receipts totaled 2,000 pesos in gold. As news spread about the reopening of the border, receipts climbed. The Sonoran state government expected to receive an average of $200,000 in gold per month from the three Sonoran ports of Agua Prieta, Naco, and Nogales. This source of revenue was essential to the rebel cause.

About that time, a small group of seven American ranchers, including Granddad, banded together to leave Sonora. Revolutionaries had put out the word that all captured gringos would be executed, and their horses, saddles, and guns confiscated. On departing, the Americans left word with friendly Mexicans to inform the revolutionaries that there were seven horses, saddles and guns the rebels wouldn't seize.

It took three days for the small band, riding at night and hiding by day, to reach the border at Palominas, west of Naco. Reaching their destination during darkness, they found that U.S. Buffalo Soldiers from Ft. Huachuca were patrolling the border to secure it from unauthorized and unwanted crossers. The small band of riders waited until morning when it was light enough to see. They were afraid that the U.S. troops guarding the boundary might mistake them for enemy and fire on them. At first light, they hailed the border guards and approached, waving a white handkerchief tied to a yucca stalk. They encountered no problems passing into Arizona territory.

Those in the group of seven included my grandfather, Marion Williams; Chick Nations; Sam Coleman; Jim and Bert Noland; and two others whose names have not surfaced. Chick got his name because he was part Indian and came from the Chickasaw Indian nation in Oklahoma. He'd been working as a cowboy for Granddad at the Santa Rosa Ranch.

In 1914, when United States forces seized the Mexican ports of Tampico and Vera Cruz, Villa looked the other way. He expressed his feeling that the United States Navy was justified in its actions, when American sailors were imprisoned falsely by Mexican soldiers.

Villa had as well a longstanding personal friendship with Gen. Hugh Scott, who became chief of staff of the United States Army.

Villa sent envoys to Washington to represent him and act as lobbyists on his behalf. He wanted to create goodwill and curry favor in high government places. One of his representatives was

Gen. Fierro, Gen. Villa, and Gen. Hugh Scott.
Courtesy of Arizona Historical Society

Gen. Felipe Angeles, who had successfully assisted the revolutionary general in many victories. Angeles was an expert artillery duelist who had been schooled in France. Villa sent him to

Washington, D.C., to persuade American authorities and elected officials that he was a friend of the United States.

Many photographs taken during revolutionary years were of Pancho Villa with American notables such as Gen. John J. Pershing, Gen. Hugh Scott, and others.

While Villa was attempting to convince the United States that he was a true friend, Venustiano Carranza, Villa's enemy, was

Obregón, Villa, Pershing, Lt. George S. Patton on right.
Courtesy of Arizona Historical Society

highly critical of Americans. Indeed, when Tampico and Vera Cruz were seized by United States forces in 1914, Carranza threatened war against the United States.

It was learned that Carranza secretly gave support to the "Plan of San Diego,"[12] a movement which planned to conquer Texas,

---

12 The Plan of San Diego was conceived in San Diego, Texas, and thus the name.

New Mexico, and Arizona in order to establish an independent government allied with Mexico. American spies also learned that the German secret service had given financing to the Plan of San Diego, which was supported by Huerta and Carranza. San Diego Plan supporters carried out brutal fights and raids against Americans across the Texas border in 1915. This was at a time when World War I was raging, and Germany hoped to precipitate a war between the United States and Mexico to divert American assistance from the allies, Germany's opponents in the European struggle.

During that time, Mexican raiders killed a number of American ranchers and murdered an American crew that was working on a border irrigation project in Texas. Mexicans also ambushed a United States cavalry trooper, cut off his head, put it on the end of a pole, and with their gory trophy paraded back and forth along the south bank of the Rio Grande, creating a horrible spectacle for American observers from north of the river.

Near Corpus Christi one night, marauding Mexicans derailed a train and passed through the passenger cars shooting Americans.

The United States government complained to Carranza, believing that he was at least nominally in control of the area where the outrages occurred. His reply was that maybe he could do something about it if the United States recognized him and declared him to be the legitimate leader of Mexico. As head of the Mexican government, he would be in a position to exert authority to stop the raids.

During those troubled days, many Americans felt that Villa was illiterate and not capable of maintaining a stable government. He was, however, able to command a substantial fighting force, even though he had lost three battles to Carranza forces, which seriously diminished his prestige.

On October 19, 1915, while Villa was en route from Chihuahua to attack Agua Prieta, President Woodrow Wilson officially recognized Carranza as head of the "legitimate Mexican government."

84

President Wilson's recognition of Carranza was over the protest of Gen. Hugh Scott, one of Wilson's most senior U.S. military commanders. Simultaneously with the recognition of Carranza, orders were issued by the United States to block all exportation of military arms or ammunition from the United States to the Villistas. In essence, Wilson's actions placed Villa in the position of bandit rather than "centaur of the north" as he had previously been recognized.

At that time, Carranza was in control of all Mexican ports on both the east and west Mexican coastlines. The effect of this was to isolate Villa, cutting off the means he needed to arm and supply his army; he was effectively bottled up in Chihuahua and Sonora.

Villa was made aware of President Wilson's recognition of Carranza while en route to Agua Prieta. He became furious. Wilson's recognition and embargoes made Villa's quest for the rich customs house at Agua Prieta far more essential.

Shortly thereafter, Villa learned that the Americans had also permitted 3,500 Mexican federal troops to be transported from Eagle Pass, Texas, to Douglas, Arizona, over American railroads through the United States to reinforce Mexican defending forces at Agua Prieta. The Mexican federals arrived at Douglas and immediately crossed over the border to Agua Prieta to assist Plutarco Elías Calles in his defense of the town.

The federal reinforcements for the defending Calles forces were composed of several trains of troops. Arriving in Douglas on October 30, the first troop train carried 850 soldiers, and a second brought 800 more troops plus women and children. In all, nine special trains arrived from Texas carrying soldiers, livestock, field guns, ammunition, arms, vehicles, and other military equipment.

While the defenses in Agua Prieta were being bolstered, Douglas, to the north, was not idle. Anticipating the possibility that Mexican troops might fire into or attempt to enter the United States over the border, the American garrison at Douglas reinforced its position by placing three regiments of infantry, a regiment of field artillery, and several troops of cavalry, a total of more than 6,500 men, along the American side of the international border. Trenches were dug on American soil adjacent to the border, extending from the eastern city limits to the first hills to the east (Saddle Gap). While the American troops were digging their trenches, both Mexican and American sightseers gathered at the border on Saturday, October 30, to watch what they anticipated would be the fight.

Gen. Thomas Davis issued a warning to all Americans in Douglas to keep off the streets and stay home until the fight ended. However, with the expectation of many things to observe, few followed this advice, and people flocked to the border to watch the fighting.

Soldiers stationed at Douglas parade past Phelps Dodge Mercantile. Note streetcar in rear. Courtesy Cindy Hayostek

As Villa marched north, bands of Villistas roamed the countryside forcing men to join Villa's army. Refugees wishing to escape Villa's wrath and conscription into his army fled to the north, with the first ones arriving in Agua Prieta on October 25. One of Villa's advance guards, under the command of Maj. Cer-

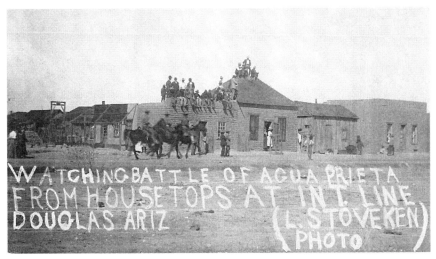

Watching battle of Agua Prieta from housetops in Douglas, Arizona.
Courtesy of Becky Stowers

vantes, skirmished with the main Villa force before surrendering to Elías Calles' forces, while some chose to cross the border into the United States. A captured Villista, sixteen years of age, who had been wounded, was taken to the Douglas Red Cross hospital where he reported that the main body of Villa's men had suffered greatly in crossing the Sierra Madre mountains on their way to Agua Prieta. It was reported that the Villistas were hungry, thirsty, and worn out. One body of troops which camped temporarily at the San Bernardino Ranch helped themselves to corn and beef; however, water was scarce.

Other Villa troops passing to the south were deprived of food because Gen. Elías Calles had seen to it that there would be none available at the Mormon colonies and environs. He had ordered closure of the Colonia Morelos flour mill, which belonged to the Lillywhite family.

With Elías Calles' troops and 3,500 reinforcements, the Mexican defenders numbered 7,500. Elías Calles' forces dug trenches with cross-firing machine guns and barbed-wire entanglements. The defenders strung barbed wire in front of their trenches to repel attacking cavalry and foot soldiers. They also laid land mines,

Lillywhite Flour Mill, Colonia Morelos.
Courtesy Arizona Historical Society

further reinforcing their defense. To top it off, three very large searchlights were set up to shine in the eyes of Villista attackers, blinding them during their night assaults. The defenders also manned 22 cannons and 28 machines guns.

On the night of November 1, 1915, Villa unleashed a devastating and fearful attack which he had successfully used in past battles. He called it his *golpe terrifico* (terrific blow). It was a ferocious cavalry charge against Agua Prieta's defenders. But trenches containing dug-in troops, with land mines, barbed wire entanglements, and interlocking machine gun fire, illuminated with intense searchlights blinding Villa's cavalrymen, all led to an early and devastating defeat for Villa. Electricity to energize the enormous searchlights was provided by the Douglas Light and Traction Company from north of the border.

The battle of Agua Prieta lasted only 18 hours. Villa, defeated and humiliated, withdrew his attacking forces and headed toward Hermosillo by way of Naco and Cananea.

One day, as a young boy, I walked the very ground on the slopes of Saddle Gap Mountain east of town where the United

Mexican trenches facing international line, Agua Prieta, November 1915.
Courtesy of Becky Stowers

States artillery was positioned. I found an unexploded artillery shell. Placing it in the metal box on the back of my motor scooter, I hauled it over the rough and bumpy dirt road five miles back to town. When Dad learned what I had brought home, he had a fit and called the local police. They in turn called the military at

Dead horses killed in front of barbed wire and trenches, November 2, 1915, day after Villa's unsuccessful attack on Agua Prieta. Douglas Smelter in background.
Courtesy of Ray Manley

Agua Prieta from Carranza searchlight tower, looking over battlefield. Three searchlights were used to blind attacking Villistas during their night attacks.
Courtesy of Becky Stowers

Fort Huachuca. A bomb squad was sent from the fort to remove the dangerous projectile, which they took to the artillery range at the military installation, where it was exploded.

During Villa's battle for Agua Prieta, Dad and several others watched the fight with binoculars from the roof of the Gadsden Hotel.

Dad related to me a particularly humorous incident about two Villistas he saw crawling on their bellies in the dirt, leading a grey horse with a pack saddle onto which they had strapped a cannon pointed over the horse's tail. Dad said, "It wasn't a very good sighting device. I believe it's one of the funniest things we ever saw. The two came up within a hundred yards of the breast-works of the Agua Prieta fortifications, and one fellow reached up and lit a fuse on the cannon. When the cannon fired, well, that horse just went end over end, because of the recoil. I guess it had a pretty heavy charge of powder in it, but didn't do much damage. They didn't try that tactic again."

"Rawhide" Jimmy Douglas owned a home at that time at the

corner of Tenth Street and D Avenue in Douglas. In 1943, he sold the house to Dad and moved to Montreal, Canada. In June of 1943, he wrote a letter to Dad saying that during Villa's attack on October 29, 1915, a bullet had come through the roof and fallen on the bed in the upstairs master bedroom. He and Mrs. Douglas went downstairs for several hours until the battle subsided, and then went back upstairs to bed.(2)

Gen. Elías Calles first learned on September 16 that Pancho Villa was planning to advance out of Chihuahua, intending to

Montreal June 29, 1943

Dear Ben:

I am so glad to have you in our house and am sure you and your family will like it.

James hopes some day to buy back his mother's piano for his boys after the war is over – so try and bear this in mind and don't sell it to anybody. It was my father-in-law's wedding present to my wife in Nov. 1891 and was delivered at the Senator Mine 12 miles south of Prescott where the Company had allowed me to build a board house that cost $1,200. It is a good piano of very good tone and sounds better than pianos now being made.

There is a hole in the ceiling in the bedroom made by one of Villa's bullets in his attack on Agua Prieta. We were in bed at the time, and moved downstairs for an hour or two.

I hope you found everything in good order and that Rose left things in good shape. You certainly got a bargain and I hope you will all be happy. Please remember me to your father and mother and to your wife.

Sincerely yours,
Douglas

Letter from "Rawhide" Jimmy Douglas to Ben F. Williams, Sr. about bullet hole in ceiling

MANY BULLETS CROSS BORDER LAST NIGHT

Combatants Across Line Careful But Still Shots Come Over Often

Buildings Are Struck and Many People Report Narrow Escapes

While bullets came over the internationla boundry line in leaden showers at times during last night's fighting across the border, army officers think that the number was very small considering the total amount of firing done. They believe both sides must have used great precautions in order to avoid sending more bullets over the line.

A number of bullets whizzed down C avenue and that thoroughfare was pretty well deserted during the early morning hours. One chauffeur tried to sleep in his auto as it stood in the street and gave up the attempt. There seemed to be certain zones of fire where the bullets were thick. At least one auto party in this city, carrying army officers, was forced to halt under the protection of an adobe wall for half an hour to get an opportunity to pass an open space. The area around the customs house seemed to be most exposed.

Hotels Struck

One bullet went through the front window of the Queen hotel on Twelfth street, made a hole the size of a goose egg, struck one wall, glanced over to the next wall and landed in the floor. Another entered a bedroom of J. A. Vestry, city ticket agent of the El Paso & Southwestern railroad, who lives at the corner of Railroad avenue and Seventh street, and passed a foot over the bed occupied by himself and son. Another bullet entered the dining room of A. W. Colton, 1300 Seventh street. One bullet is said to have entered the window of a bedroom occupied by two young men in the Taylor home, 931 Ninth street. A number passed close to the Y. M. C. A. Owing to danger to the oil tanks of the Texas Oil company, Local Manager Shappard ordered all employes to keep away from the plant. Bullets are said to have struck the Gadsden hotel and the Phelps-Dodge building.

Lelevier Gets Scene

Gustavo G. Lelevier, owner of a printing establishment on Tenth street just west of the Y. M. C. A. said this morning that he owes his escape from being struck by a bullet to the fact that after coming through the front window of the shop it struck the tin plate of a job printing press and was deflected upward and above

(Continued on Page Eight)

Article in *Douglas Daily Dispatch*, November 2, 1915.
Courtesy of Arizona Historical Society

Bullet went through roof

The Williams home, showing where bullet came through roof

capture Agua Prieta. Villa had previously suffered a humiliating and devastating defeat in the battle of Celaya in April of 1915,[13] six months prior to his planned attack on Agua Prieta. It was during the battle of Celaya that his esteemed and elite cavalry, the dorados, were almost all killed or wounded. Wanting to recoup from his Celaya defeat, Villa had returned to Chihuahua, where he regrouped and assembled between 10,000 and 13,000 troops. He planned to seize Agua Prieta and its customs house, then proceed by way of Naco and Cananea west to seize Hermosillo, the capital of Sonora. He wanted the valuable and income-producing Mexican customs house at Agua Prieta to help support his war effort.

Elías Calles received word that Villa had left Casas Grandes on September 16 with a column of 13,000 troops and 40 cannon. Along with the cannon were caissons and pack animals carrying artillery shells for his guns.

---

13 See Chapter 6.

Villa's column had to pass through El Pulpito Canyon in the Sierra Madre mountains, and proceed on to Colonia Oaxaca, Colonia Morelos, San Bernardino, Gallardo, and Agua Prieta. It was estimated that of Villa's force, 1,500 to 2,000 were cavalry.

Gen. Elías Calles estimated that 18 to 22 days would be required for Villa to reach the plaza at Agua Prieta. He analyzed the situation and carefully devised the plan utilizing trenches and barbed wire, similar to battle techniques then in use in Europe during World War I.

The preparations and battle hold great interest for me because I grew up in Douglas across the border from where the engagement was fought.

The plan was dated October 22, 1915, and provided for the town, comprised of 33 city blocks of residences and a population of 800, to be divided into four sectors. From Armando Elías,(3) I was able to obtain a sketch of the battle plan for the defense of Agua Prieta in November of 1915. The plan's architect, Gen. Plutarco Elías Calles, was later to become President of Mexico from 1924 to 1928.

Gen. Plutarco Elías Calles, successful defender of Agua Prieta.
Courtesy Fototeca FAPEC-FT

In command of the first sector to the east was Col. Lazaro Cárdenas, who was to become president of Mexico in 1934. His "volunteers" were from Cumpas, a town south of Agua Prieta. They had six machine guns.

Commanding the second sector to the southeast was Lt. Col. Florencio Fimbres with volunteers from Nacozari[14], also a town south of Agua Prieta, armed with rifles and four machine guns.

---

14 Granddad's Santa Rosa Ranch was only ten miles from Nacozari.

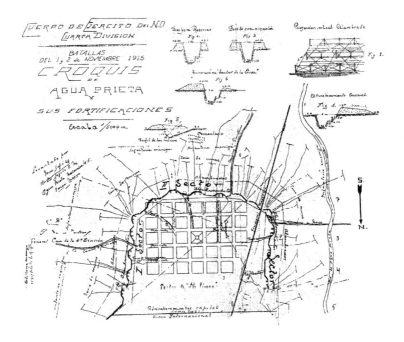

Gen. Plutarco Elías Calles' battle plan for the defense of Agua Prieta.
Courtesy of Armando Elías

Commanding the third sector was Col. Antonio Ancheta, with troops from Pilares, adjacent to Nacozari, who manned six machine guns.

The fourth sector was located adjacent to the U.S. international boundary line, and was commanded by Col. Silvestre Quevedo, with troops to protect against any piercing of the first and third sector by Villistas along the U.S. border.

In addition, Gen. Elías Calles established a general reserve of troops commanded by Col. Angel Camargo.

The plan called for installation of land mines in front of the barbed wire barricades, which the enemy would have to cross prior to reaching the barbed wire barricades.

Should the Villistas penetrate the barbed wire, which was designed to stop troops and horses, the defenders would then be protected by a secondary defense of trenches to protect against infantry and horsemen as well.

Machine guns were spaced approximately 30 meters apart and positioned so as to provide a withering crossfire to stop both infantry and cavalry.

Provided in the plan, as well, were underground areas for installation and protection of Elías Calles' artillery. The trenches were connected in order to provide easy communication from one to another.

During the battle, it was reported that Calles ordered his band to play spirited military marches while Villistas attempted unsuccessfully to penetrate the town's defenses.

Calles' artillery in action.
Courtesy Ray Manley

Plutarco Elías Calles' post-battle report quoted an article from the *Douglas Daily Dispatch* reporting Villa's braggadocio that it would take only two hours to take the town and occupy the plaza of Agua Prieta. When asked by the reporter how many cannons he had, Villa's response was, "Count them when you hear them thundering. There are plenty."

PRESIDENT IS CONSIDERING PLAN FOR USING TROOPS TO PROTECT CITY FROM VILLA

Funston May Be Empowered to Take Radical Steps if Lives On This Side Are Again Endangered; Villista Army Swings Over to Southwest and Calles Sends Out Column to Capture Cannon and Harass Retreating Column: Callistas Say Enemy is Moving to Naco But Generally Believed It Is Resting for Renewal of Attack.

WASHINGTON, Nov. C====The president and Secretary Garrison are considering authorizing Gen. Funston to invade Mexico if necessay to protect Douglas.

For the first time since the Villa army entered Sonora, Gen. P. Elias Calles took the offensive this morning, his troops evidently being encouraed by the failure of Villa to take Agua Prieta in his first attack.

Douglas Daily Dispatch, after battle on November 1, 1915.
Courtesy of Arizona Historical Society

Douglas Daily Dispatch, November 2, 1915.
Courtesy of Arizona Historical Society

After his defeat at Agua Prieta, Villa proceeded west to Naco, where he forcibly detained two American doctors, surgeons for the Cananea Copper Company, who had offered their services to treat his wounded troops. Villa extorted food and supplies (1,500 head of steers and 175 horses and mules from the Cananea Copper Company) on threat of executing the doctors. He accused them of being Yankee spies (not true, of course). The copper company paid the ransom for the doctors' release.

When I was a boy living across the border from Agua Prieta, I remember four burial markers in the center of Seventh Street and Seventh Avenue in the eastern part of Agua Prieta. The markers were placed at the graves of four federal soldiers, one of whom was Gen. Cruz Galvez. The four were killed by Villa's troops on November 1, 1915, and buried where they fell. After many years, the graves were removed from the middle of the street, and the bodies reinterred in the Agua Prieta Municipal Cemetery.(4)

The battles of Celaya and of Agua Prieta marked the beginning of the end of Villa's military prominence.

Monument in center of 7th Street, Agua Prieta, where Gen. Cruz Galvez was buried where he fell in Villa's attack on November 1, 1915. Agua Prieta presidente (mayor) José Ortiz third from left.
Courtesy of Cezar Careaga

11

PANCHO VILLA'S GOLD

In 2003, my cousin Hector Salazar owned a ranch in the foothills of the Buenos Aires mountains east of Bacoachi, Sonora. Bacoachi is a village that the Spaniards established on the banks of the Sonora River more than 400 years ago.

Hector recalls that when he was a little boy Pancho Villa's troops camped in the yard of Ramón Salazar, Hector's father, whose home was located in Bacoachi. Hector related to me that he saw Villistas camped for three or four days in front of his childhood home. They wore leather bandoliers loaded with cartridges.

Their commander was Gen. José Rodriguez, who along with Villa had been defeated at the battle of Agua Prieta on November 1, 1915, after a short, intense fight. Villa suffered the loss of many of his followers during the Agua Prieta fight.

After his defeat at Agua Prieta, Villa ordered Rodriguez to break off from the main body and proceed south to Bacoachi to await further orders. Villa was meanwhile moving west with his main force to seize Hermosillo, the Sonoran state capital.

Another member of the family who lived close to Ramón was his cousin Adolfo Salazar. A number of Villistas pitched camp in the yard of Adolfo's home, where they stayed for more than a week.

After the troops left, Adolfo noticed newly disturbed areas of dirt in his back yard. It was obvious that somebody had dug holes and filled them with fresh dirt. Adolfo removed the dirt and found two coffee cans full of gold coins. They had obviously been buried by Villa's men, hoping to return one day and recover the gold.

Why was the gold buried? Think for a moment how difficult it would have been for a Villista to secretly carry the gold with him. If he was mounted, all he had was perhaps saddle bags, already full of gear required for his travel. Maybe he might have a small bedroll tied behind his saddle as well. It would not be easy to transport heavy gold coins without being discovered. If a trooper was marching on foot, the added weight of heavy gold would be like dragging an anchor.

Adolfo was very secretive about his newfound wealth. He didn't want anyone to know he had come into what in those days was a fortune.

It became Adolfo's good luck, for possession is nine-tenths of the law, as they say, and Adolfo kept the gold and his secret well.

Years later, in 1957, when Dad and I officed together at the Gadsden Hotel in Douglas, I recall Hector visiting Dad and bringing with him a coffee can full of gold coins. At the time, private ownership of gold was illegal in the United States, since in 1934, President Franklin Delano Roosevelt had called in gold. The Gold Reserve Act had been passed on January 30, 1934. It authorized the U.S. Treasury Department to seize all gold held by Federal Reserve Banks, and make private possession of gold illegal except for "legitimate" purposes (jewelry, artwork, and industrial and scientific uses).

On January 31, 1934, FDR issued an executive decree changing the price of gold from $20.67 an ounce to $35 per ounce. Gold maintained its price of $35 per ounce until August 15, 1971, when President Richard Nixon announced that the United States would no longer convert dollars to gold at a fixed value, thereby abandoning the gold standard. This permitted the price of gold to "float" and reach an international trading value. Subsequently, on December 31, 1974, President Gerald Ford signed a bill legalizing the private ownership of gold coins, bars, and certificates. As I write this story in July of 2010, gold is quoted at $1,210 per ounce.

Hector, fearful of illegally owning the gold, asked Dad what he could do with the precious gold coins. Dad told him, "Hell, I'll buy them."

So they struck a deal. Dad paid Hector the agreed amount and took possession of the treasure.

You're wondering what happened to the contents of the coffee can. So am I. I never saw the can or its contents again after that day in my father's office. I can only surmise that the gold at one time belonged to Pancho or his men.

Mexican Thug Who Has Defied United States and American Victims

The dead—

A. L. RITCHIE, hotel proprietor.

WALTON WALKER, United States customs rider.

MILTON JAMES.

MRS. MILTON JAMES.

J. S. DEAN.

C. C. MILLER, druggist.

J. J. MOORE, merchant.

W. R. WALKER, Playas, N. M., guest in Central Hotel.

UNIDENTIFIED CHAUFFEUR.

MARK A. DEBBS, sergeant machine gun troop.

FRANK T. KENDALL, horseshoer.

GENERAL FRANCISCO VILLA

PAUL SIMON, corporal.

JOHN NIEVERGELT, band sergeant.

HARRY WISWALL, corporal, Troop G.

FRED A. GRIFFEN, private, Troop K.

THOMAS BUTLER, Troop F.

The wounded—

JESSE P. TAYLOR, Troop F.

THEO. KALZORKE, Troop L.

MICHAEL BARMAZEL, machine gun troop.

JOHN YARBROUGH, Troop K

JAMES VENNER, Troop M.

JOHN KEOGH, Troop G.

C. C. BENSON. Lieut., Troop G

Front page, *Santa Fe New Mexican* newspaper, New Mexico, March 9, 1916.
Courtesy of Bisbee Mining & Historical Museum

12

"PANCHO VILLA INVADES THE U.S."[15]

Other front page headlines from the same newspaper:

"BANDITS BURN AND KILL IN COLUMBUS"

"DEATH TO AMERICANS, PANCHO'S CRY; WANTS TO CHOKE HATED GRINGO"

"AMERICAN TORN FROM WIFE'S ARMS, SHOT LIKE A DOG AND ROASTED"

En route to Agua Prieta for the fateful battle, Villa's army set up camp on the Mexican side of John Slaughter's ranch, seventeen miles east of Douglas, Arizona. Villa and his men had come from Casas Grandes across the Sierra Madres, and were tired, thirsty, and starving. They had had no beans, flour, or meat, and very little water during the previous two days. It did not take long for them to devour Slaughter's cornfields and fifty head of his cattle without consulting the ranch owner.

---

15 Headline, *Santa Fe New Mexican* newspaper, March 9, 1916

Slaughter Ranch, the San Bernardino

Slaughter stood on the front porch of his San Bernardino Ranch house and watched his beef and corn disappear down the throats of Villa's soldiers. After muttering to himself for a while, John finally told a cowhand to bring his shotgun and his horse. When his wife, Viola, asked where he was going and what he intended doing, he answered, "I say, I say, I'm gonna ride down and jump old Pancho Villa!" (Slaughter always began his sentences with "I say, I say.")

With his shotgun resting on the saddle horn, 74-year-old Slaughter rode right through Villa's army and up to the general himself. He and Pancho knew one another, as Villa had been a guest at the ranch a number of times. John had a serious talk with old Pancho and when he returned, it was with his saddlebags full of nice, shiny $20 gold pieces which Villa had paid for Slaughter's cattle and corn.[16]

My grandfather, Marion Williams, had known Slaughter since Marion's childhood days when they both lived in Tombstone. Later, they had dealings at Granddad's Santa Rosa Ranch southeast of Cananea.

Granddad was 91 years old in 1962 when interviewed by Don

---

16 This account comes from Ben Traywick's book, *That Wicked Little Gringo.*

Robinson, a reporter for the *Arizona Daily Star*. The purpose of the interview was to get some perspective about Slaughter and to learn from someone who knew what life was like back in the early days of the West. Histories of Arizona and Sonora were always of interest to researchers and historians as well.

The newsman wrote of Williams' purchase of the San Bernardino Ranch in 1937 from Slaughter's widow, Viola. Granddad knew the famed rancher, lawman, legislator, and banker, about as well as anyone living at the time of the interview.

Williams remembered: "Boy, you can sit here and ask questions all day and never really know how men like me and Slaughter fixed it so you could drive in a cushioned automobile from Tucson here in less than four hours." [The drive can now be done in two hours on a modern highway.]

Williams recalled: "Slaughter wasn't a bad man at all . . . but he was a very dangerous man . . . very quick with a pistol. He killed 12 men in the 10 years he was sheriff–and they all had it coming. And don't think that most of them weren't damn tough.

"When John Slaughter went after a man, he brought him back–and most of the time, the man was dead.

"I was just a boy when I first knew Slaughter," Williams continued. "He didn't pay much attention to me, but once when he was sheriff he offered to put me through school over at Tombstone if I'd come and milk his cow twice a day. I didn't take him up on it."

Williams recalled how Slaughter once recovered his stolen saddle from a man who died from a Slaughter-injected dose of "lead poisoning."

"I was in town [in Naco, a town just across the border in Mexico, south of Bisbee]. A man called Peg Leg Finney was gambling and losing and he went and sold a team and buggy that didn't belong to him and after losing that money, he took my saddle from a livery stable, stole a horse, and took off. I was left bareback with a long ways to go."

The theft was reported to the Cochise County authorities. A

couple of days later, Williams got word from Sheriff Slaughter that he had "captured" Peg Leg.

"I hear you lost your saddle," the sheriff said. "Identify it."

Williams described his Gallup Frasier saddle with a broken saddle string, and soon he wasn't bareback any longer. Peg Leg had been shot dead and was buried in the little cemetery on Slaughter's San Bernardino ranch. "Quite a few people got their stuff back," Williams related.

Arthur Finney
Inquest notice of death

Inquest report for Arthur "Peg Leg" Finney, September 20, 1898.
Courtesy of Ben T. Traywick

Tough men living in tough times.

After striking camp at the San Bernardino, Villa's army continued west to Agua Prieta, where his troops suffered their stunning defeat in a short but intense battle. During the battle, on the United States side of the border, one U.S. civilian and one Army soldier were killed, while several civilians were wounded[17].

Camp Douglas, ca. 1915, before being renamed Camp Harry J. Jones.
Courtesy of Cochise County Historical Society

To add insult to painful injury, Elias Calles' military band played stirring marches during the futile attack. They played from the protection of their trenches.

Villa's humiliating loss at Agua Prieta was a great emotional letdown for the general. In addition, the depressing news that President Woodrow Wilson had publicly declared U.S. recognition of Carranza, Villa's enemy, greatly affected his judgment. He had attempted in many ways to garner President Wilson's favorable nod over his enemy, Carranza. Villa was angry and felt betrayed by Wilson's actions. It is believed that the bad and unexpected news of President Wilson's endorsement of Carranza reached

17 Camp Douglas was established in 1910. On November 2, 1915, Corporal Harry J. Jones was guarding the United States Customs House when he was struck by a bullet. The bullet wound caused his death a few days later. Camp Douglas was renamed Camp Harry J. Jones in February 1916 in honor of the only American soldier who was killed as a result of Villa's attack on Agua Prieta. In 1960, my wife, Daisy, and I built a house at 2100 Ninth Street in Douglas on the site of that old military camp. When excavating for a swimming pool, we found an old pint whiskey bottle complete with stopper; also a brass collar insignia from a soldier's uniform.

Villa at Colonia Morelos, a Mormon colony forty-five kilometers southeast of Agua Prieta, before the battle for Agua Prieta.

Villa became a vengeful enemy of the United States and all gringos from that day forward.(1)

After the defeat at Agua Prieta, Villa's army began to shrink in size. Desertion from the ranks became a common occurrence. At one time, a group of 250 cavalrymen all left Villa to join the opposing army.

From Agua Prieta, Villa moved west to Naco, where he split his forces. Gen. José Rodriguez, with almost half of Villa's troops, veered southerly to Bacoachi on the Sonora River, while Villa's main force traveled on to Cananea and Hermosillo. After suffering defeat at Hermosillo, General Villa turned east with his weary troops toward Batuc, Sonora, 90 miles southeast of Hermosillo.

Men were beginning to desert in increasing numbers. The glorious days of his old dorados and their invincibility were gone. Villa was down to seven artillery pieces when he reached Batuc, a small village south of San Pedro de la Cueva. There local inhabitants informed him that because of the precipitous downgrades and cliffs leading to the river, it would be impossible for his artillery to pass.

Learning this, Villa's men dismantled the cannons and packed the more portable parts on mules for transport to San Pedro. At a point west of Batuc, the disassembled artillery, consisting of seven cannons, with a small escort, veered off to the north from the main body to proceed to an easier passage by way of San Pedro de la Cueva, intending to rejoin the main body at Batuc. The main body proceeded south down the mountains to the old colony at Batuc.

On December 1, 1915, people at San Pedro saw dust on a ridge to the northwest. A number of horsemen were approaching, something that had become distressingly familiar to them during past months. Marauding bands of one revolutionary faction or another, but mostly representing no one but themselves, had made

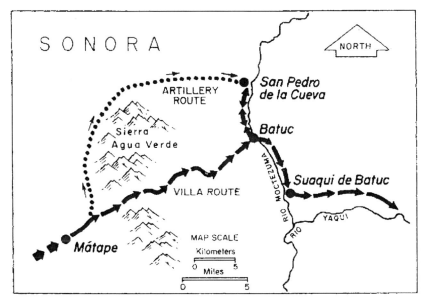

Map of Villa's line of march to San Pedro de la Cueva.
Copyright by the Western History Association, printed by permission. The map first appeared in the article "Massacre to San Pedro de la Cueva: The Significance of Pancho Villa's Disastrous Campaign," *Western Historical Quarterly* 8 (April 1977): 124 and 139

a habit of sweeping through the defenseless village demanding money, valuables, and food. The townspeople had little enough as it was. While these plundering groups seldom harmed anyone or damaged property, they caused tremendous economic hardship.

No one knows why the men of San Pedro chose this occasion to take action, but they did. Believing the advancing riders to be just another gang of raiders, they decided to ambush them before they reached the village. It never crossed their minds that they could be soldiers under the command of Francisco Villa.

As many as ninety men from San Pedro hid along the northwest approach to the town. As the Villistas rode past, the villagers opened fire. Using a motley collection of light arms, they were able to surprise Villa's men, killing several of them. The artillery escort returned the fire, mortally wounding one San Pedro defender.

Shouting to each other, both sides soon discovered that a mistake had been made, and the shooting stopped as quickly as it had begun. Explanations were hastily exchanged and apologies given. The escort sympathized with the villagers' plight and readily understood why they had done what they did.

Col. Marcario Bracamontes, the leader of the escort, was in a dilemma. Villa was already waiting for him in Batuc, and the skirmish had consumed valuable time already. Bracamontes was a native Sonoran, already saddened at the blood and destruction he had witnessed in his own state during the past month. Now he feared that San Pedro would be the scene of another disaster. He suspected how Villa might react. The colonel feared his commander's present mood, and was aware that if provoked, Villa was capable of savage ruthlessness.

From San Pedro, Bracamontes dispatched a messenger to Villa at Batuc, just a few miles away. He told the courier to inform the general of the artillery's progress, explaining there had been a slight delay in negotiating an irrigation ditch. He was to say nothing of the ambush. The villagers were warned as well to say nothing about the incident.

But almost before the skirmish ended, a villager hurried to notify Villa of their mistreatment by his troops. Thus, Villa learned of the matter only minutes after it was over. But the *campesino*'s (peasant farmer's) lament failed to kindle any sympathy; instead, the informer cowered in the face of Pancho's tirade. Hearing his men had been attacked, Villa flew into a rage. His sensibilities deserted him. Without even waiting for confirmation from his own soldiers, he ordered an immediate march to San Pedro, to make an example of those who dared to interfere with Pancho Villa. Raving like a maniac, he vowed to destroy the town and every person in it.

On Villa's arrival, he had the small town completely bottled up, and the men and boys herded into separate buildings. He ordered that all men, women, boys, and girls be executed because of the attack upon his artillery column.

After much pleading, and the intervention of a Catholic priest, Father André Abelino Flores, thirty-five years of age, Villa relented, and decreed that only the men and boys fifteen and older who were able to shoot a rifle would be put against the wall.

While Father Flores was relating his failed mission to the people, one told of learning that prisoners could be released by payment of 3,000 pesos each. Everyone contributed what they had, which amounted to only 7,000 pesos.

The village women then pleaded with Flores to approach Villa again. Although reluctant to do so, the priest made another try to intercede on behalf of the menaced boys. Flores took the 7,000 pesos and approached Villa. As he neared, Villa drew his pistol and shot Father Flores between the eyes, killing him instantly. Villa took the 7,000 pesos from Flores' body. Before the priest was killed, Flores' father tried to keep the bandit from shooting his son. Villa leveled his pistol, and shot him in the head, as well. The old man fell unconscious, but survived. The bullet had glanced off his skull without killing him. The aged man, although left for dead, recovered to tell the awful story to the world.[18]

The executions continued until all the grown men and boys had been executed. They died in groups of four, shot down in front of Villa's firing squads.

The incident at San Pedro de la Cueva was one of the more distasteful of Villa's military exercises in the eyes of the outside world. Little public information was garnered about the massacre other than a few brief articles in the Douglas, Tucson, and El Paso newspapers.

Thomas H. Naylor, an ethnohistorian and research associate with the Arizona State Museum in Tucson, wrote an essay in which he described Villa as follows:

---

18 The story of the executions was related in both the *Arizona Daily Star* and *Arizona Daily Citizen* on January 4, 1916, bearing a Douglas dateline.

Widows and orphans of San Pedro de la Cueva, after Villa executed all men and boys 15 and older. Note crosses in background.
Courtesy of Armando Elías

"In Sonora, Villa lost his capacity for responsible leadership. He became instead a callous, vindictive demon . . . [He] sank to depths he never reached again . . . [He] methodically massacred nearly eighty of his own countrymen; he coldly murdered blameless non-combatants, the exact class of people for whom he ostensibly risked his life in the revolution."

There were other atrocities. On January 10, 1916, American mining engineers who had been guaranteed safe conduct on a Mexican railway by the governor of Chihuahua set off for the Cusi Mining Company works some distance away from Chihuahua City. Near the village of Santa Isabel, Villistas stopped the train and forced eighteen Americans to get off, where they were summarily shot, stripped of clothing, and their bodies mutilated. Although Villa was not present at the killings, United States officials charged the savagery to him.

News of the wanton murder of the Americans reached the United States, and on January 14, Americans in El Paso began attacking the city's Mexican quarter in reprisal. Gen. Pershing deployed troops to the area to avoid wholesale slaughter.

At a small Sonoran colony called La Colorada,[19] Villa and his followers murdered sixteen Chinese. Some of the victims were

19 La Colorada lies between Hermosillo and Batuc.

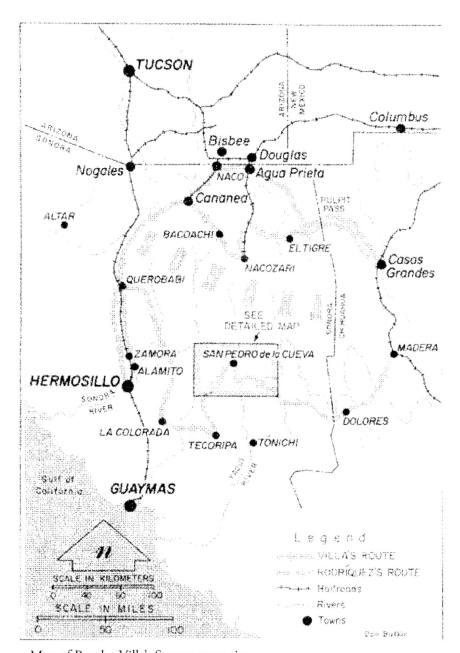

Map of Pancho Villa's Sonora campaign.
Copyright by the Western History Association, printed by permission. The map first appeared in the article "Massacre to San Pedro de la Cueva: The Significance of Pancho Villa's Disastrous Campaign," *Western Historical Quarterly* 8 (April 1977): 124 and 139

shot, some were hanged, and some had their bodies pulled apart by horses.

Villa and his diminishing forces continued to travel easterly to Nacozari.[20] It was while they were camped there that Villa dispatched one of his captains with an escort of mounted and armed men to seize 300 head of cattle from my grandfather's Santa Rosa ranch, as told in another chapter in this book.

Proceeding eastward on March 8, while his troops rested at Boca Grande southwest of Columbus, New Mexico, Villa sent Col. Cipriano Vargas and another officer to scout the military garrison and village of Columbus. Vargas returned at midday, reporting that there were no more than 40 soldiers on the post, and that while scouting, he was never challenged[21].

Arriving on the outskirts of Palomas, Chihuahua, on the Mexican side of the border, Villa's troops prepared for an attack into the United States. Prior to battle, Villa divided his force of 484 men into two columns, and at 4:20 a.m. on March 9, 1916, his troops attacked the small, sleeping village during darkness. Residents recall hearing the Villistas shouting, "*Viva Villa, Viva Mexico, muerte a los gringos.*" (Viva Villa, Viva Mexico, death to the gringos). The invaders were running on horseback and wildly firing their rifles while setting fire to numerous homes and stores.

In his unpublished memoir, Alva Anton Fredrickson related how prior to the Columbus attack, a friend, one of the Fernandez boys from La Ascención, a village next to Colonia Diaz, almost rode his horse to death coming out [of Mexico] the day before the raid to bring word that Villa's people were planning to raid Columbus.

Frederickson writes that his father took Fernandez to see Col. Slocum, the officer in charge of the U.S. troops at Camp Furlong[22]

---

20 Many of Villa's forces began to question their leader's judgment, and deserted in big groups, as indicated earlier.

21 From *Fort Huachuca: The Story of a Frontier Post*, by Cornelius C. Smith, Jr., 1976.

22 Camp Furlong housed 350 troops of the 13th Cavalry Regiment, and was located south of Columbus between the town and the Mexican border. Columbus was located three miles north of Palomas, Chihuahua, the Mexican port of entry. Palomas was also the Mexican headquarters for the Palomas Ranch, a 2,270,000-acre spread in which my father, Ben F. Williams, Sr., owned a one-fifth interest in the 1940s. A house in Columbus served as the ranch's American headquarters.

Col. H.J. Slocum on left, Columbus, New Mexico.
Courtesy El Paso Public Library, Aultman Collection

south of Columbus, where he was merely laughed at.

Col. Slocum stated, "Why, nobody would dare invade the United States!"

"He didn't even go so far as to place troops on outposts to warn of approaching bandits." Frederickson writes: "He didn't do a thing. So as a result, well, a little bit after midnight, . . .Mexican troops were already in the town. They had bottled up all the American soldiers in their barracks where they could do nothing . . . Mexican troops cut the telegraph lines on the railroad and began looting the town and setting fire to quite a few of the buildings. One building belonged to Uncle Kim Lemond, who owned a grocery store and general mercantile." He writes, "I'll never forget, when [the fire] reached the barrels of kerosene, which everybody used for lights, when one of those blew up all of a sudden, you'd really get a big glob of light in the sky and you could see what was going on."

Frederickson relates that the men of the town and soldiers began to defend themselves and actually launched a counterattack. "I'll tell you, Pancho Villa's forces paid a horrible price for coming across the line. They had so many dead and dying that the next morning they made huge funeral pyres and burned all the bodies.

"Of course," Frederickson continued, "father was real furious over the thing because it shouldn't have happened at all. If the American troops had done what they should have done, Columbus would have never been raided, because the fight would have taken place down at the border.

"And, of course, there was no way they could have got that far because we had enough troops there that they could have routed them and kept them in Mexico. Well, father was so disturbed he went up to Fort Bliss and saw the commanding general . . .and reported what had happened, and he said, 'That man [Col. Slocum] ought to be cashiered out of the Army.' I've forgotten the name of the general, I met him too, but he said, 'There is no way you can touch that man. He belongs to an old, longstanding Army family, and they'll just move him around and keep him out of the limelight for a few years, and then he'll just go right along.'"

Columbus is three miles north of the United States-Mexico border. Between Columbus and Palomas, Chihuahua, lay Camp Furlong, a military camp which was occupied by elements of the 13th U.S. Cavalry. Many of the camp's officers were absent at the time of the attack. Some had gone to Deming to attend a dance, while others were away playing polo in El Paso.

To further hinder the defense of the military camp and town, the soldiers' weapons and ammunition were locked up in the guardhouse.

The Villistas killed 18 people (nine American civilian men, one woman, and eight troopers of the 13th Cavalry).

At least 67 Villistas were killed during the battle, and a number wounded. Among the cavalry's weapons were Maxim machine guns manufactured in France. They constantly malfunctioned, making the defense of Columbus even more difficult, although it was reported that on that early March morning, 20,000 rounds were fired through the guns at Villistas.

It is believed that one of the reasons for Villa's attack on Columbus was to seek revenge upon Sam Ravel, the owner of a local

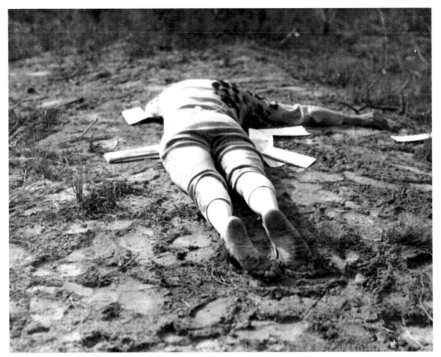

U.S. soldier where he fell, Columbus, New Mexico. Note bare feet–he
didn't have time to put his boots on.
Courtesy El Paso Public Library, Aultman Collection

general mercantile. Ravel supposedly had been paid $50,000 by
Villa for rifles and ammunition which were never delivered. A
further reason, as mentioned earlier, was that Villa was incensed
over President Wilson's declaring in October open U.S. support
of Carranza, Villa's enemy. At the same time, Wilson ordered an
embargo on the shipment of arms, ammunition, and war materials
to Villa. Villa wanted revenge.

One officer reported that after the alarm was given, the
command promptly assembled and soon gained control of the
situation. Villa admitted a loss of 190, which speaks well for the
discipline and morale of the American command.[23]

The raiders looted the town, burned a number of buildings
(including the hotel and local bank), and rode off with an estimated 100 U.S. Army horses.

---

23 The number of Mexicans killed and wounded varies from writer to writer and among historians.

Columbus, New Mexico, after the raid, showing burned area.
Courtesy of Dutch and Cherie Salmon, High-Lonesome Books,
Silver City, New Mexico

Douglas Meed, in his book *Soldier of Fortune*, wrote that the raiders had less luck attacking the 13th Cavalry than they did the village's citizens, though certain anecdotes show citizens' courage—and rage. When a dozen raiders burst into the cook's shack, they were doused with boiling coffee, and one was decapitated by an enraged baker who took the attacker's head off with an ax. Other cooks retaliated against the attackers with swinging meat cleavers and Army-issue potato mashers, which could crack a skull like an eggshell. "One raider was brained by a trooper on kitchen patrol swinging a baseball bat like a berserk Babe Ruth," wrote an unknown Army officer.

Troopers, although their ammunition was locked up, were able to grab rifles and break into the guardhouse to obtain ammunition and their French-made machine guns. Troopers quickly set up the guns, blasting away at raiders outlined against the flames of the blazing business district. Columbus became too hot for the raiders as the sky began to lighten with the coming dawn. Grabbing anything they could carry, they scrambled to their horses and retreated across the border.

As a bugler blew "Boots and Saddles," troopers, some still in their underwear, grabbed Springfields, bandoliers of ammunition, and their saddles and rushed to the stables.

The battle lasted until 6:30 in the morning, when a force led by Maj. Frank Tompkins, bleeding from a knee wound, initiated a pursuit into Mexico, chasing the withdrawing Villistas. Tompkins led a squadron of troopers from the 13th Cavalry after Villa. On fresh cavalry horses, they outran many of the raiders and shot them down during a fifteen-mile chase. Then, low on ammunition and with no water, Tompkins called a halt, and the troopers rode back to Columbus. His force numbered only 29 men. They pursued 2,500 Mexicans under the leadership of Villa a distance of 15 miles, killing 75 Villistas and capturing many horses and supplies. During the engagement, Tompkins lost nary a man.

Maj. Tompkins later wrote that in the pre-dawn hours of March 9, 1916, "the infamous Mexican revolutionary Pancho Villa and some 484 men crossed the United States/Mexico border and carried out a stunning surprise attack on the unsuspecting New Mexico border village of Columbus. During the raid, the Villistas killed 18 Americans (ten 13th Cavalry troopers and eight civilians, one of whom was a woman)."[24]

Tompkins continued: "Following its initial surprise and disarray, the Army garrison fought back and after two hours of street fighting, succeeded in driving Villa's troops from the village. In the process, the 13th Cavalry, with rifle and machine gun fire killed an estimated 62 Mexican attackers and wounded another 25 or so."

Lt. John P. Lucas, 13th Cavalry, commenting on the Columbus battle, said later, "We were also criticized for taking so few prisoners. We did take . . . five wounded men, and they were . . . later tried and hanged for murder."

In reviewing the unpublished memoir of Alma Anton Frederickson[25], I found mention of the fact that during the 1912 Mexican

---

24 Reports vary on the number of casualties.
25 Frederickson died in Globe, Arizona, on July 24, 2002, at the age of 92. He was buried in the National Memorial Cemetery of Arizona in Phoenix.

American cavalry with dead Villista, Columbus, NM.
Courtesy of Dutch and Cherie Salmon, High-Lonesome Books,
Silver City, New Mexico

revolution, "it became important that the people in Colonia Diaz had to leave there [Chihuahua] because of the harassment that was going on, and so they left and went out to Hachita, New Mexico. Traveling by wagon and carrying whatever personal possessions they could, they crossed into the United States, where they were met by U.S. cavalry troops who escorted them to Hachita, New Mexico, where they resided in tents provided by the government."

From Hachita, they moved to Columbus, New Mexico. Frederickson's grandfather was a carpenter who contributed to the building of the community. He helped build the school and a number of brick buildings, for which he provided not only the laying of brick, but carpentry services as well. He assisted in the construction of an ice house to accommodate ice brought in by rail from El Paso. He also installed an electric generating plant, which greatly helped the community in its growth for that day.

Later, he bought and operated the electric plant.

Frederickson spoke of community LDS meetings, and remembered his mother playing music on a reed organ brought out of Mexico by the family.

Frederickson's memoir reflects a distinguished military career. He was promoted to full colonel prior to his Army discharge. At one time he served under Gen. George S. Patton, commander of the U.S. Third Army in Europe.

Frederickson knew that Patton excelled in the use of the saber, and even had designed one for military use. Frederickson also studied the use of the saber, and received a medal as a saber expert.

Knowing that Patton was going to call upon his command, Frederickson took out his medal and put the decoration on his uniform. The next day, sure enough, Patton inspected Colonel Frederickson's unit. Frederickson recalled in his memoir, "He [Patton] had the funniest, squeakiest voice, and in that funny, squeaky voice he said, 'Where in the hell did you get that decoration for the saber?' I looked the old boy right in the eye, and I said, 'The same damn place you got yours, sir!' And that's all it took, we talked about everything under the sun from that time on. We talked for about thirty minutes before the general left."

After the Columbus raid, in a report issued by Gen. Pershing relative to the attack on Columbus, he reported to his superiors, Gen. Frederick Funston, Commanding Southern Department; Gen. E.A. Garlington, Inspector General, U.S. Army; Gen. Tasker H. Bliss, Assistant Chief of Staff, U.S. Army; and Gen. H.L. Scott, Chief of Staff, U.S. Army; as follows:

> Colonel Slocum seems to have made every endeavor to obtain accurate information of the whereabouts and intentions of Villa. The information received from the usual Mexican sources was unfortunately, credited, when as a matter of course, under the circumstances, it was entirely unreliable. From headquarters, both of the Department

and of the Brigade, the information regarding Villa's exact whereabouts and his intentions were not such as to cause any particular alarm in Colonel Slocum's mind, although he did reinforce the troops patrolling the border line.

Articles appearing in the *Washington, D.C., Evening Star*, March 10, 1916, and the *New York Times* on March 19 consisted of a letter written by M.M. Marshall to his father, E.J. Marshall, President of the Palomas Land and Cattle Company, whose two-million-acre property lies on the Mexican side of the line south of Columbus. The *Star* article assumes that the military at Columbus probably had no night guards in the camp, and certainly no exterior guards, and then goes on to say in the most fatuous manner that:

"It is one of the first principles of military work to guard against surprise. The necessity for security and information is a cardinal principle of the soldier's training, and seemingly this principle was forgotten at Columbus."

In the letter to his father, young Marshall stated that it was the United States Army that should have been blamed. They were forewarned by two Palomas employees (foreman Fondille and Antonio), who told the military of Villa's whereabouts and his line of march. He further relates that the Army unit at Columbus was "extremely lucky" in having so few of its soldiers killed in the raid. He states that it was just luck. Col. Slocum was overconfident and thought that Villa would never dare attack American troops in the United States.

Marshall's letter also related that at about 8:00 on the morning of Tuesday prior to the raid, "McKinney [of the Palomas Ranch] and myself sighted about 500 men in the process of making camp. They were unsaddling and starting to make coffee. McKinney wanted to go up and talk to them, but I told him, 'Arthur, please don't go because they may be Villistas.' I told him that if they were Villistas, he would surely be killed."

McKinney disregarded Marshall's warning and accused him of cowardice for not accompanying him into the camp. McKinney then rode toward the camp in company with one of the Palomas' Mexican cowboys.

Young Marshall rode to warn other Palomas cowboys not to go into what he thought could be a Villista camp. Corbett later stated he would join McKinney, disregarding Marshall's admonition. Corbett then rode directly into the camp, where he was seized. The Villistas had sighted Marshall and his other cowboys and laid chase. They were able to escape the Villistas and ride into Columbus on the night of March 7.

Young Marshall further related that on arriving in Columbus, he notified the colonel in command of the U.S. troops of Villa's approach. The colonel sent Marshall back to scout and locate Villa's band and report back to him.

On the night of Wednesday, the 8th, Marshall reported to the colonel that about 500 to 700 men were on the Casas Grandes River heading toward Columbus.

The following morning the Villistas attacked Columbus.

A Negro water foreman from a neighboring ranch, named Bunk, who was a captive at the time Villa took foreman McKinney and Corbett, made the following report on the death of the two men:

McKinney rode right into the camp of Villa, and as he rode through inspected the horses quite thoroughly. The Mexicans took him captive, and soon after took Corbett, who came into camp of his own accord. Their capture was reported to Villa, who at the time was not in camp. Villa ordered them hung. McKinney laughed and joked with the men as they were making preparations, and shook hands with me and some of the men as he was pulled upon the limb of a tree, remarking that there was only one chance to die.

Corbett also shook hands with me when he came into camp, and at that time realized his time had come. He took his death like a brave man. O'Neil, the cook, was also killed. The cook was laid on the ground, and 60 horses lined up to run over him, he was fighting every second.

The second horse went over him, but as the third humped he grabbed the stirrup and swung himself up behind the rider. He had almost choked to death the Mexican rider when a bullet pierced his heart and he fell.

Bunk and a Mrs. Walker, who was also a captive of Villa at the time of the murder of McKinney and Corbett, escaped after Villa and his men left the camp on their way toward Columbus.

Col. Frank Tompkins, in his book, *Chasing Villa*, outlines statements of Gen. Pershing, Gen. Frederick Funston, Inspector General E.A. Garlington, Maj. Gen. Tasker H. Bliss, Chief of the General Staff, and H.L. Scott, Chief of Staff, all who commended in one way or another the conduct of Col. Slocum, and in particular the men of his command who resisted the Villistas and chased them from Columbus into Mexico, killing a number of Villa's troops.

I should like to point out that Maj. Frank Tompkins, who led the chase into Mexico, was at the time a subordinate officer under the command of Col. Slocum. I ask you to examine the various statements to determine in your own mind who was most culpable in the Columbus affair.

James W. Hurst, in his book *The Villista Prisoners of 1916-1917*, wrote:

"The eighteen Villista prisoners were taken to Deming. Nine of them were subsequently hanged, and the other nine were hurried off to prison in Santa Fe."

Another author, Andrew Gulliford of Middle Tennessee State University, stated, "Fifteen Mexicans taken prisoner were tried by jury and hanged in Deming, New Mexico."

Haldeen Braddy wrote, "Military officials succeeded in holding from the irate citizens thirteen Villista prisoners in their custody, these being shortly conveyed for their protection to Deming, New Mexico. A trial of sorts occurred there nearly three months later, and two of the guilty marauders met death by hanging."

James A. Sandos reported that "Ninety of Villa's followers were killed and seven captured." He went on to say that sixteen more raiders were captured by the punitive expedition, tried and imprisoned, but later pardoned by New Mexico governor Octaviano Larrazolo, who stated that the men were merely following orders and therefore not subject to American jurisprudence.

So you can see that many writers and historians have differing versions of the number and disposition of captured Villistas, as well as numbers killed and wounded.

Villa's army at the time of the Columbus raid was more an armed mob than trained soldiers. Many had been conscripted after being threatened with execution by firing squad if they didn't "join" the bandit leader. Such options left little choice. The Columbus militants were a far cry from Villa's *dorados* of former years.

The Villa engagement was the last U.S. cavalry campaign using horses and mules. Subsequently, animals were replaced by automobiles and trucks.

Almost immediately after the attack on Columbus, at noon on March 9, the Army chief of staff, Maj. Gen. Hugh L. Scott, was informed of the raid by telegraph. The new Secretary of War, Newton D. Baker, was being sworn into office. Baker's first official act was to set in motion the punitive expedition into Mexico. Baker notified Maj. Gen. Frederick Funston, in a communication: "You will promptly organize an adequate military force of troops, under the command of Brigadier General John J. Pershing, and will direct him to proceed promptly across the border in pursuit of the Mexican band which attacked the town of Columbus, New Mexico on the morning of the 9th inst. . . ."

The official dates of the American expedition in pursuit of

Gen. Pershing leading "flying column" into Mexico, chasing Villa in 1916.
Courtesy of Dutch and Cherie Salmon, High-Lonesome Books,
Silver City, New Mexico

Villa indicate that it commenced on March 14, 1916, and ended on February 7, 1917.[26] Some 10,000 men "pursued" Pancho Villa and his bandits into Mexico.

It is interesting to note the swiftness with which U.S. military forces responded after the raid on Columbus. Records derived from Fort Huachuca, Arizona, originally a cavalry post established in the late 1800s, show that news of the Columbus raid first came to the attention of the Huachuca authorities at 11:00 a.m. on March 9 when the regimental adjutant, Capt. Samuel MacPherson Rutherford, received a phone call from the local telegraph operator. He relayed the news to the regimental post commander, Col. W.C. Brown. Upon receipt of the information, Col. Brown immediately ordered that his troop commanders be notified at once with instructions to "hold their troops in readiness for orders."

---

26 During the campaign, Pershing's troops were trained and toughened up in preparation for their subsequent service in Europe as part of the U.S. expeditionary forces during World War I.

Subsequent directives came within half an hour from cavalry brigade headquarters in Douglas, directing the command to proceed to Douglas at once, "ready for service in the field."

By 4:00 p.m. that same day, elements of the 10th Cavalry (Buffalo Soldiers[27]) departed from Fort Huachuca while the post band played "The Girl I Left behind Me" "to the tearful goodbyes of loved ones and the chagrin of those troopers left behind."

The Buffalo Soldiers adopted as their own war cry, "Villa, dead or alive!"

On its way to New Mexico, the regiment made its first stop at Hereford on the evening of March 9 and, going by way of Douglas and the Slaughter and Hood ranches, arrived at the rendezvous point, the Culberson Ranch in New Mexico. There the Buffalo Soldiers assembled, and later met in Mexico with other U.S. troops from Columbus and El Paso's Fort Bliss.

There, folks, is the story of Villa's attack on the United States. He was never caught and never punished for his murderous, dastardly and surprise acts of war and atrocities committed against the United States.

And here's a footnote:

In 1916, the Palomas Land and Cattle Company owned a large ranch in Chihuahua west of Palomas, where Villa's people had killed an American the day before the raid. Maj. Tompkins tells us that a Mexican named "Antonio," an old employee of the Palomas Company, appeared in Columbus and reported that on the morning of March 7 (two days before the attack), at the Palomas ranch the foreman by the name of McKinney saw Villa and about 500 of his men in camp on the Casas Grandes River. Maj. Tompkins also reported that on "Tuesday, March 7, 1916, McKinney was killed at Boca Grande in the forenoon."

In 1941, the ranch was acquired by five partners, one of whom was my father, Ben F. Williams, Sr.

Along with land, cattle, and other personal property was a

---

27 The Buffalo Soldiers consisted of members of the 9th and 10th Cavalry---Negro soldiers with a distinguished history of service.

Browning automatic rifle (the famed "BAR"), used so effectively by U.S. troops in World War II after its development in 1918. Also included was a 10-gauge pump shotgun. The weapons were carried in the automobile of the Palomas ranch superintendent during revolutionary days, which didn't end until 1929. Dad surrendered the BAR in 1943 to the FBI because it was unlawful for civilians to own machine guns. The guns had been stored in the Palomas office in Columbus.

As a teenager, I spent several days and nights at Columbus in the house that was the American headquarters of the Palomas Company. In the 1940s, the outside plastered adobe walls of the building still bore pockmarks from Villista bullets fired during the attack of March 9, 1916.

13

THE MILITARY AT SAN BERNARDINO RANCH

V illa's attack on Columbus caused the Army to increase
their manpower at John Slaughter's San Bernardino
Ranch by two companies. During the Mexican revolutions, the
outpost was used as a base for patrolling the international border.

Military squad tents on mesa, Slaughter Ranch, 1916

From the San Bernardino, ten-man patrols scouted to the west, while other ten-man units patrolled all the way to the Animas Valley in New Mexico. They looked for troublesome revolutionaries, but seldom encountered any.

When it was rumored that Villa was going to return and attack Agua Prieta again after the Columbus raid, the camp's troop size was increased by both infantry and cavalry to a force of 600 men.

Duty at the San Bernardino outpost was usually boring. Troopers had little to do when not on patrol other than care for their horses and equipment.

To help ease the monotony of duty, soldiers invited young ladies from Douglas to join them for horseback rides and picnics at the beautiful springs, which flowed with a great abundance of clear, warm water. John Slaughter had drilled nine artesian wells which produced a never-ending flow of waters. The water from one well was warm enough to comfortably bathe in. Slaughter installed a large standpipe which cast water from the well like a huge bathroom shower.

First class tent service at the Slaughter Ranch outpost.
Courtesy of Harvey Finks, Johnson Historical Museum of the Southwest

There were enough people at Slaughter's ranch and surrounding countryside to justify a small store and post office. The post office operated during revolutionary days, from 1906 until it closed in 1918. The store carried staples such as flour, rice, *frijoles*, and raw coffee beans. To the great delight of the women

Women visiting the Slaughter Ranch in 1916, enjoying the warm water artesian well.
Courtesy of Harvey Finks, Johnson Historical Museum of the Southwest

and children shopping at the store, bright, gaudy cottons and hard candy were featured.

In 1918, two cavalry officers, Capt. David H. Blakelock and 2nd Lt. George J. Lind, while hunting rabbits a few yards north of the border, were surrounded by Mexicans, who seized and took

John Slaughter at his artesian warm water well, 1909, Slaughter Ranch.
Courtesy of Harvey Finks, Johnson Historical Museum of the Southwest

them south of the line to an adobe building where they were held prisoner.

Soldiers at the camp learned of this and, disregarding orders, crossed the border and rescued the officers. In the course of the rescue, two Mexicans were shot and killed, creating an international incident which festered for several years.

After 1918, the San Bernardino outpost was used primarily for rifle practice and training marches. Many maneuvers were made by foot soldiers from the Army camp in Douglas, a four-hour march away.

John Slaughter loved to gamble and attended almost nightly card games at the camp across the pond from the ranch house. Officers from the camp on the mesa were also hosted by Slaughter from time to time. The games provided a welcome break for camp officers from outpost boredom.

John Slaughter, with ever-present cigar.
Courtesy of Harvey Finks, Johnson Historical Museum of the Southwest

Often, Slaughter would have horses saddled for his wife, Viola, and a lady riding companion for an evening ride.

Slaughter would then ride his horse over to the army camp on the mesa for a good card game.

Viola didn't want her husband to gamble, so he assured her

that the stakes were very small. Many times they were not; on one occasion it was reported that a trooper lost $80 in one evening, a handsome sum at the time, for it constituted one month's pay.

While writing this tale, I ran into an old friend, George D. Stephens IV. The Stephens ranch was located immediately east of the San Bernardino, which had belonged to my grandfather.

George's father (also named George) and John Slaughter were close friends and neighboring ranchers for many years.

I asked George if he still owned the 30.06 Springfield rifle that I recalled from high school days.(1) He said he did, and that he had reconditioned it and replaced the barrel so it was serviceable. He told me the story of its acquisition–how a Stephens cowboy found the weapon next to the Black Draw sometime in the 1940s.

Here is the tale of the 30.06: During Pancho Villa's revolutionary days, the U.S. cavalry maintained an encampment on the mesa located immediately east of the pond at the Slaughter ranch headquarters. The camp was just a couple of miles west of the Black Draw.

George related how the cavalry developed maneuvers whereby, in anticipation of an attack by Villa forces, U.S. troops would retreat north along the Black Draw to a given point in order to draw in attackers. Once invading forces were in pursuit in that area, other mounted cavalrymen would ride in from high ground and spring the trap, bottling up the enemy.

The U. S. soldiers and Villistas never actually engaged in battle because Villa's troops didn't cross the border at the San Bernardino. But had they done so, the cavalry was prepared to take them on.

It was on one such maneuver that a Springfield rifle was dropped, sometime around 1915, only to be found by one of Stephens' cowboys in the 1940s.

14

THE CÁRDENAS INCIDENT

John J. Pershing was born in Linn County, Missouri, on September 13, 1860. After working as a schoolteacher, he attended the military academy at West Point. Graduating from the Point, he became an instructor at the University of Nebraska, where he taught military science and studied law. He was awarded a law degree and thereafter was assigned to frontier duty fighting Indians.(1)

Gen. Pershing acquired his nickname of "Blackjack" when he was assigned to the Tenth Cavalry, a regiment made up of black troopers. They became known as Buffalo Soldiers, dubbed that by the Indians because their hair resembled the dark, curly hair of the buffalo.

On January 20, 1914, Pershing was transferred to Fort Bliss just outside of El Paso on the Mexican border. He was charged with the responsibility of supervising U.S. Army units patrolling the border. After Villa's infamous and devastating raid on Columbus, New Mexico, Blackjack was ordered to lead approximately 10,000 American troops into Mexico in pursuit of the renegade. (2) Pershing's command was not acquainted or familiar with the alien Chihuahua terrain. It had been reported to Pershing that he would be entering the Mexican republic into a desolate, barren, and sandy plain with rolling foothills. His troops would be

U.S. troopers on horses in Chihuahua, chasing Villa.
Courtesy of El Paso Public Library, Aultman Collection

encountering tropical heat, cold snows, and fierce, hostile winds.

Pershing's expedition relied on guides who knew the country and its people. They ranged from cowmen, half-breeds, ranch bosses, and adventurers who had fought either against or for Villa, to gunfighters and gamblers. As a scout and guide, no one could fit the bill better than Emil Holmdahl, a seasoned, tall, lanky individual who wore a large Colt .45 strapped to his gun belt.

He knew the country well, spoke Spanish like a native, and more importantly, knew Villa. Holmdahl had fought against the Mexican general, and also had fought for him. Having been denied a commission in the U.S. Army because of age, Holmdahl nevertheless offered his services to Blackjack Pershing.[28]

A young, able, and eager member of Pershing's expeditionary staff was 2nd Lt. George S. Patton, Jr. He was to become famous in World War II as a formidable commander of U.S. forces in North Africa fighting German Field Marshall Irwin Rommel, famed as "the desert fox." He later achieved more recognition for his successful campaign in Europe commanding American soldiers of the Third Army in the memorable Battle of the Bulge.(3)

Patton, whose duties as aide to Gen. Pershing were administrative in nature, was dying to see action. With the passage of time, he was finally able to convince Pershing that he was the man to go on a special mission to the San Miguelito ranch in Chihuahua. He was to determine whether or not one of Villa's most trusted confederates and a former leader of Villa's elite squadron of dorados, Gen. Julio Cárdenas, was visiting his wife at the family hacienda. The detail's mission was to find and capture or kill the Villista general and his aides.

On May 15, 1916, Patton's small command consisted of three large Dodge touring cars, two civilian drivers, ten infantrymen armed with Springfield Model 1903 rifles, and two civilian scouts. One of those scouts was Emil Holmdahl. As the small force entered the village of Rubio in Chihuahua, Holmdahl spotted some Villistas among a number of men loitering in the town's plaza. They were men he had soldiered with in campaigns against Huerta while he was fighting for Villa. He whispered to Patton, "They are Villistas. I recognize them, and they are pretty bad men."

Patton's patrol, including Holmdahl, proceeded to the San Miguelito Ranch eight miles north of Rubio, where Gen. Julio Cárdenas, a former leader of Villa's elite squadron of dorados, was rumored to be. Cárdenas' wife and mother were living in the large hacienda at the time. A plan of attack was formulated whereby several men would cover the windows of the hacienda,

---

28 For more on Emil Holmdahl, see Chapter 18.

and Holmdahl and a driver would remain in one car to cover the hacienda's north side.

The three cars drove up to the ranch buildings. Patton, the feisty young shavetail, jumped out of his auto, rifle in hand, while the other men rushed to their assigned positions. Patton was later to write, "When I was about 15 yards from the gate, three armed men dashed out on horseback . . . I drew my pistol and waited to see what would happen . . . ."

The three horsemen broke from the ranch at breakneck speed. Patton shouted for them to halt. Instead, the three armed riders turned and charged Patton, the leader yanking a rifle from his saddle scabbard and opening fire. All three horsemen shot at Patton, one bullet hitting the ground in front of him, throwing gravel in his face. At 60 feet, Patton calmly held and squeezed five rounds from his .45. One round hit the leading horseman in the arm; he fell from his saddle and ran toward a doorway as Patton reloaded. [Note: This was his famous pearl-handled .45 Colt revolver, which Patton carried for years.]

The second horseman, desperate to escape, spurred his horse toward freedom, passing in front of Patton's six-shooter. Patton recalled what an old Texas Ranger had told him. The best way to stop a horseman is to shoot his horse. He did so with one shot. The horse and rider fell, with the rider arising and firing rapidly. Patton and his other troopers shot and brought down the third rider with rifle fire.

At the sound of gunfire, Holmdahl, on the other side of the building, came on the run, shooting rapidly. The man wounded in the arm had fallen to the ground and, lying face down, lifted his head, raising his left hand in a gesture of surrender. Holmdahl walked toward him. The wounded man recognized Holmdahl as a former Villista officer, and with great effort raised his pistol and fired. The bullet missed Holmdahl, whistling past his ear. Holmdahl drew his pistol and coldly shot his old saddlemate, Gen. Julio Cárdenas, through the head. One of the drivers later stated that Holmdahl was an adventurer who killed for pleasure.

Patton and his men placed the bodies of the three dead Villistas spread-eagled, one over each car's hood, tying the bodies securely to the vehicles. Julio Cárdenas was known to Holmdahl and later, the other two men were identified as Col. Gildardo Lopez and Pvt. Juan Garza.

The three automobiles with bodies over their hoods returned to Pershing's headquarters that afternoon, creating quite a sensation. They drove through the camp like a band of proud deer hunters displaying their kills. Later, an old cavalry colonel, looking at the bodies of the Villistas, remarked, "Look at the dirty bastards; look at the blood and guts on those dirty bastards."

And thus Patton's legend and the nickname of "Blood and Guts" were born. It is said that Patton's ivory-handled revolver thereafter bore notches on its left ivory grip.

For his action, Patton was promoted to the rank of 1st Lieutenant. He was 31 years old.

Later, Patton wrote the following letter of recommendation for Holmdahl:

> Headquarters United States Troops
> Somewhere in Mexico
> May 20, 1916
> To Whom it may concern:
> This is to certify that Mr. E.L. Holmdahl, was the Government Scout with the U.S. Troops under my command in an engagement with Villa Bandits, at San Miguel Ranch, Chihuahua, Mexico, on May the 14th. I highly recommended Scout Holmdahl, for his coolness, courage and efficiency while under fire, he personally killed General Julio Cárdenas, and Colonel Gildardo López, in a pistol duel. At that time Holmdahl fought in the open, without cover of any kind and shot with great accuracy and deliberation his action being that of a man at target practice.

I also wish to recommend him to any brother officer, who may wish a man who is thoroughly familiar with Mexico and its people or in any position of trust, as he is most reliable, and a Good Soldier.

(Sgd) Geo. Patton.

1st Lieut 10th, U.S. Cavalry

This is the same George Patton who became the famous proponent of armored warfare and whose Third Army fought in the Battle of the Bulge at Bastogne; the same general who, after years of exposure to battle in harm's way, died as a result of a jeep accident on December 21, 1945, in Europe. He was 60.

After Holmdahl's service to Pershing's expeditionary forces, Gen. Pershing wrote to the Attorney General of the United States the following letter:[29]

I desire to recommend executive clemency in the case of E.L. Holmdahl, charged with violation of the neutrality laws on the Mexican border and sentenced to eighteen months imprisonment. An inquiry into the facts of this case leads me to believe that Holmdahl should not be held to more than a technical violation of the neutrality laws.

Moreover, as a scout with the Punitive Expedition into Mexico, he performed service which should entitle him to the Government's consideration. I trust you will give this request such consideration as you may deem advisable.

On July 13, 1917, Holmdahl was granted a full and unconditional pardon of pending federal charges by President Woodrow Wilson. He immediately enlisted as a private in the 6th Engineer Regiment. Although at first turned down for physical reasons, he was later approved for military service because of the intervention of political heavyweights who favored him. Several days after his

---

29 See Chapter 18 on Emil Holmdahl for background.

enlistment, he was promoted to 1ˢᵗ Sergeant.

Two weeks later, his unit departed for France to serve in World War I. Within weeks, Holmdahl was promoted to 2ⁿᵈ Lieutenant and then thereafter quickly to 1ˢᵗ Lieutenant. Holmdahl returned from France after suffering shrapnel wounds to his stomach.

It was reported that his military service records were lost in a fire at the Federal Documents Depository in St. Louis, along with much of the documentary evidence of his World War I service. Records of so many of his exploits were lost.

15

BAPTISM BY FIRE: THE ARMY AIR CORPS

Pershing's campaign into Mexico in March of 1916 saw the first military use of airplanes by the United States. The unit designated as 1ˢᵗ Aero Squadron was unofficially organized in Texas City, Texas, on March 5, 1913.(1) At the time, Gen. Victoreano Huerta was rattling the saber in Mexico, fomenting revolution. The United States was evaluating a possible military intervention if security of the U.S. or its citizens was threatened.

Some enterprising and forward-thinking pilots felt that the new airplanes of that day could be of military use in Mexico should the United States become militarily involved.

Our southern neighbor was experiencing troubled and tumultuous times after the collapse of Porfirio Diaz's thirty-year reign as the country's absolute, dictatorial leader.

It was not until after Pancho Villa's attack on Columbus, New Mexico, on March 9, 1916, that U.S. use of airplanes in war became a reality. It was then that the 1ˢᵗ Aero Squadron, with a complement of eight Curtiss JN-3 aircraft, was activated for duty. The squadron, commanded by Capt. Benjamin D. Foulois[30], was

---

30 Subsequently, Capt. Foulois climbed the ladder of command until his retirement as a Major General.

1st Aero Squadron, #53 at Casas Grandes, Chihuahua, March 1916.
Courtesy CafePress.com

ordered to join Gen. John J. Pershing as an element of his expeditionary force into Mexico in pursuit of Pancho Villa.

Prior to Mexican service, the air unit was sent to Columbus on March 12. Very shortly after arrival, on March 16, it flew its first mission in Mexico under the command of Capt. Foulois. The group flew south of the U.S. border to Colonia Dublan near Casas Grandes, its new base in Chihuahua, Mexico. Dublan was to become the squadron's Mexican base of operations until April 22, when the unit returned to home base, all aircraft having been lost or rendered inoperable.

Flying conditions in Chihuahua were extremely difficult. Dry desert winds and heat caused wooden propellers to delaminate, making it necessary for pilots to carry spare propellers when flying extended missions.

A serious shortcoming of the planes was the fact that they were underpowered and couldn't fly above 10,000 feet, the altitude required to fly over the high Sierra Madre mountains of western Chihuahua.

The 1st Aero Squadron's TO&E (table of organization and equipment) consisted of 11 officers, 84 enlisted men, 8 Curtiss JN-3 "Jennies," 10 trucks, and a touring car. The unit's missions were made more difficult because it was not supplied with accurate maps or reliable compasses. The planes carried no machine guns or effective bombs, and their engines were underpowered, making them inadequate for the purposes intended.

They were primarily used to carry dispatches to places where trucks and animals proved too slow. Several aircraft also "bombed" ground forces and installations with grenades during combat engagements. One or two planes were shot down or damaged by enemy ground fire from Winchester rifles. The canvas-covered planes proved to be generally ineffective. Mechanical problems took the highest toll. In the wild and rugged Chihuahua terrain, aviation mechanics and spare parts were in critically short supply, if available at all. During the few weeks' operation, from March 9 to April 20, five of the eight planes were wrecked, and one, which was damaged in a forced landing at a point too distant from any repair facilities, was abandoned after being destroyed by its crew.

By April 20, only two airplanes, numbers 45 and 53, remained, and these were in such poor condition that they were unsafe for further field service. They were flown back to Columbus and ultimately condemned and destroyed.

One of the squadron's outstanding flight officers was Capt. Foulois. He and his fellow officers believed that aviation was indispensable to military operations, and that airplane design should provide for greater speed, dependability, and weight-carrying capacity. Both commissioned and enlisted personnel felt that the knowledge gained from their experiences should result in more rapid and efficient development of the aviation service.

The squadron reported at the end of April that all but two planes had been lost, adding that the squadron's flying officers were continuously called upon to take extraordinary risks in every reconnaissance flight made while on duty in Mexico. Capt. Fou-

1st Aero Squadron being refueled in the field in Mexico.
Courtesy of El Paso Public Library, Aultman Collection

lois noted, "All officers thoroughly appreciated the fact that the failure of their airplane motors, while flying through mountainous canyons and over rugged mountains, would invariably result in death. No officers died, but there were several close calls."

The following is from a transcript of the handwritten personal diary of 1st Lt. Herbert A. Dargue, Signal Corps USA, pilot of Curtiss JN-3 #43, 1st Aero Squadron. It gives a firsthand view of the pilots' performance in the expedition and describes Dargue's part in effecting the change in status of the aviation section of the Signal Corps:

Wed. April 19 - Flew with Willis as observer in 43 from San Antonio [in Mexico] at 5:25 A.M. Scoute [sic] roads leading to Chihuahua and city of Chihuahau [sic]. Took several pictures. Attempted to follow road west ot [sic] city and got in among hills that we could not get out of on account of down currents. Finally motor began to vibrate and lost power so we were unable to keep up. In an effort to turn to the right and get back down the valley the machine lost so much power engine going down to 1200 R.P.M., and altitude was lost on account of down currents. We smashed into a hillside 45 degree slope and wrecked completely, the machine turning over on both of us.

I was fortunate in getting out uninjured though severely shaken up and exhausted. Willis was pinned under the fuselage, both feet being caught between the engine bed and gas tank. The machine fell at 7:15 A.M. Willis got a 3 cornered cut back from the left temple and then down in back of the left ear about 4 inches on a side. The whole piece of scalp was loose from the head. I bandaged it up with our two 1st aid packets and managed to stop the bleeding. He lay down in the shade while I collected what we needed to carry with us. I had a hard time hacking the machine away so as to get his feet loose. His left leg just above the ankle was badly bruised and sore. At 9:35 we started on our hike in the mountains touching a match to what was left of 43 as we departed.

The squadron's service from March 15 to August 15, 1916, saw 540 flights, for a total flying time of 345 hours and 43 minutes. The distance flown during the period totaled 19,553 miles.[31]

---

31 The squadron was to see action in Europe in World Wars I and II. Later, one of its functions was to train U-2 pilots such as Francis Gary Powers, whose high-altitude reconnaissance plane was shot down by the Russians on May 1, 1960.

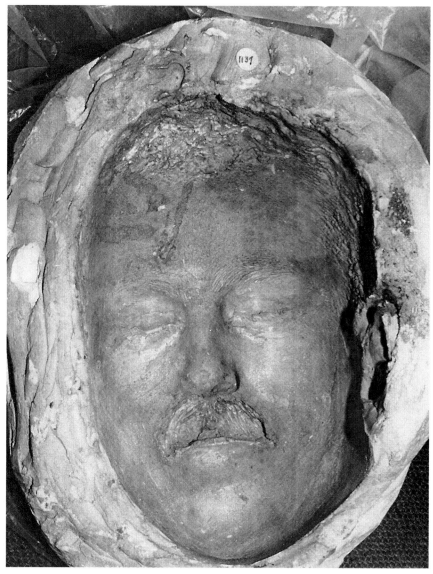

Pancho Villa's death mask.
Courtesy of Radford School, El Paso, Texas

16

PANCHO VILLA'S SKULL

This is the story of the disappearance of Pancho Villa's skull. Just remember, if it rambles a bit---well, so did Pancho's skull.

Just a few days after my father's book[32] was published in 1984, I received telephone calls from newspaper reporters for the *New York Times*, *Wall Street Journal*, *El Paso Times*, and *Arizona Republic*, each asking what I knew about Pancho Villa's skull.

Their inquiries related to one of the stories in Dad's book. It was about Pancho's skull and the mystery surrounding its disappearance. I told the reporters I was aware of nothing more than what had appeared in the book. Actually, I did know more, from stories I had heard him tell many times over the years. But I didn't feel I had the time to engage in what I felt could become an endless and time-consuming exercise. My law practice and job as mayor of Douglas were very demanding in those days, and if I had become involved in the controversy, my time and politics would have become greatly compromised.

George H.W. Bush was running for vice-president then in a hotly contested race, and there were political detractors who

32 *Let the Tail Go with the Hide*

wanted to discredit him and his campaign by linking his family to the severance and theft of Villa's skull. Stories were circulating that the men of the Bush clan[33] were members of the Skull and Bones, a Yale University secret society,[34] and that Pancho Villa's skull resided in the "tomb" of the society on the Yale campus.

Dad lived in El Paso when he was a young man in the mid-1920s. Working for the Gutta Percha & Rubber Manufacturing Company, a subsidiary of Robins Conveying Belt Company of New York, his job was selling conveyor belting, hose, and industrial diamonds to the mining industry in Mexico. His work took him to company offices and mines throughout the Mexican republic. Some were located in such rough and remote places that they could be reached only on the back of a horse or mule.

His trips into Mexico sometimes took several weeks, but he felt at home in the rugged country and comfortable with its people, having been born in 1901 in the small Mexican village of Bacoachi,[35] located on the Sonora River south of Cananea, Sonora.

Dad's father was American, his mother Mexican. The first language he learned was Spanish. His exposure to English was at the age of eight, when he was sent to live with his grandmother and aunts in Beloit, Kansas. None of them spoke Spanish. While in Beloit, Dad attended elementary school, learning to speak, read, and write English. It was tough being immersed in school with all Anglo kids and not knowing a word of English.

With the passage of time, however, he became completely bilingual, speaking both Spanish and English with equal ease and without accent. His education was later enhanced by attending high school in Douglas, Arizona, and White's Preparatory School in Berkeley, California. Two years of college at the University of California at Berkeley followed.

During those years, my grandfather, Marion Williams, owned the Santa Rosa Ranch where Dad lived and worked when not at-

33 Prescott Bush, George H.W. Bush, and George W. Bush.
34 The Skull and Bones secret men's fraternity was founded at Yale University in 1832.
35 Bacoachi was founded by Spaniards in 1649. The name comes from the Opata Indian language and means "surrounded by water."

tending school. The Santa Rosa was located ten miles northwest of Nacozari, a mining town seventy miles south of Douglas. The Moctezuma Copper Company, a subsidiary of Phelps Dodge Corporation, owned and operated a large copper mine and mill at Nacozari.

Living near Nacozari, and being exposed to the mine and mill, helped Dad become acquainted with the mining industry.

He started as a salesman for the Gutta Percha Company, headquartered in El Paso, while in his early twenties and single. Dad found living quarters at the Davista Apartments, from which he later moved to the Toltec Club.

The Toltec Club was founded in 1902 by influential El Paso business leaders as a residential club for men. It employed a housemother who oversaw and chaperoned social activities, which included young ladies. Members attended the club's swanky social

Toltec Club, El Paso, Texas.
Courtesy of El Paso Public Library, Aultman Collection

events formally attired in "tails." The Toltec Club remained one of the top social clubs in El Paso until the 1930s, when it faded away.

It was at the Toltec Club in the 1920s that Dad and Major Emil Holmdahl[36] became acquainted. Both were bachelors. Although Holmdahl was eighteen years older than Dad, they became good friends and often went to dinner together in both El Paso and Juarez. They usually dined at the Central Café in Juarez, a fancy nightclub which featured a nine-member band. Although several weeks might pass between meetings, the two enjoyed their social encounters, sharing stories and experiences of life in Mexico.

Fast forward to 1926. Pancho Villa is now dead. Dad was still making extended trips throughout Mexico in his job for the Gutta Percha Company. On one of his trips in February of 1926, he passed through Parral, Chihuahua, where he stopped for the night. It had been a long, tiring day, and he was looking forward to a warm shower and a good meal at Dinty Moore's hotel.

Checking in, Dad was welcomed by an old friend, Alex Espinosa, the desk clerk, who said, *"Buenas tardes, Señor Williams."* (Good afternoon, Mr. Williams.) *"Usted es amigo de Emil Holmdahl?"* (Are you a friend of Emil Holmdahl?)

"Sí, porque me pregunta?" (Yes, why do you ask?)

"Porque esta en el juzgado." (Because he's in jail.)

"Why is he in jail?" Dad asked.

"He's accused of robbing Pancho Villa's grave and stealing the general's head. They're holding him incommunicado. No visitors."

The next day, Dad went to see the town's mayor, Antonio Martinez, whom he had known for several years. After the usual pleasantries, Dad asked, "Antonio, I understand you're holding Major Emil Holmdahl in jail incommunicado. I'm told he's charged with robbing Pancho Villa's grave and stealing his head. Is this so?"

"That's right, Ben. You know Parral is a small town, and as mayor, I make it my business to know what's going on and who

---

36 See Chapter 18.

comes and goes in this place. I can't think of anybody else new in town who might have done such a horrible thing."

"Antonio, may I have a written order granting me permission to visit the man? We're good friends. I've known the major for some time in El Paso."

"Okay, Ben," Mayor Martinez stated, handing my father a written order signed in his own hand. It was permission for Dad to see the prisoner. To make it official, he stamped the document with the seal of the mayor's office.

"Antonio, have you confronted Holmdahl about the matter?"

"Yes, of course, but he strongly denies having anything to do with the grave robbery. Ben, do you know where the jail is?"

"I sure do," Dad said, thanking Martinez for the order permitting him to visit his friend.

By the time Dad got to the jail, it was nighttime and dark. The mayor's order provided for visitation at any time.

On his arrival at the jail, Dad showed the order to the jailer and told him he wanted to see the American prisoner. He was directed to a cell, where he found Holmdahl, who had been locked up for three days. The prisoner was sitting in a dingy cell illuminated by a single candle burning on a table. When the jailer admitted Dad, he was greeted by Holmdahl, "God, Ben, am I glad to see you!"

"What are you doing here, Major?" asked Dad.

"You know the charges against me?"

"Yeah. You're charged with digging up Villa's body and cutting his head off. Is that right?"

"That would be the most stupid thing in the world. Why in hell would I want Pancho Villa's head?"

"That's a damn good question. Then you had nothing to do with it?"

"Hell, no. The whole thing is ridiculous. Can you get me out of here?"

"Yeah, I think I can," Dad said.

"Ben," Holmdahl said, "please get this damned jailer to bring me a big tub of hot water, some soap, and a kerosene lamp so I can see. Then bring my bag from the hotel, with a razor and a change of clothes. I haven't had a bath since they put me in here. I want to shave and clean up."

Dad gave the jailer a five-peso gold piece and asked him to bring hot water, soap, and a lamp. After leaving the jail, Dad went to Dinty's hotel, where he gathered Holmdahl's clean clothes and a razor to take to him.

The next day, Dad once again met with the mayor. He inquired of him, "Have charges been filed against Major Holmdahl?"

"No," the mayor responded.

"Well, then," said Dad, "you're going to have to release him. You've had him in jail for over three days, and you know the law. One can't be jailed for over 72 hours without being officially charged with the commission of a criminal offense." Dad was right.(1)

"You're right, Ben," said Presidente (Mayor) Martinez. "As much as I hate to let him go, I'll issue an order for his release today."

That evening, Dad and Major Holmdahl went to dinner and agreed to meet for breakfast around 6:00 or 6:30 the following morning. A few minutes after 6:00 a.m. the next day, Dad went to the major's room and knocked on the door. There was no response, so he knocked again. The night porter heard the knocking and approached Dad, telling him that if he was looking for Major Holmdahl, he had checked out in the middle of the night.

Dad asked, "Did he say where he was going?"

"*No. No mas salio. Pago su cuenta y se fue.*" (No. He just paid his bill and left.)

It was a month before Dad returned to El Paso. Upon his return, he went to the El Paso Club, located on the top floor of the Hussman Hotel, for lunch. There he encountered Holmdahl.

The major greeted Dad, saying, "Ben, I've been waiting for you. I knew you'd come back sooner or later. I'm glad to see you. Let's have a drink."

It was during prohibition; sale of liquor was prohibited, but club members had lockers where many kept bottles of liquor. Holmdahl went to his locker and returned with a bottle of whiskey. The two sat down at a corner table. Seated and enjoying a whiskey and water, Holmdahl said, "Ben, I have a confession to make. You got me out of that jail in Parral."

"Yeah," Dad responded.

"I told you I had nothing to do with cutting off Villa's head. Well, I did. I took the head and disposed of it. I was paid $25,000 plus expenses for the job. Half of the money is yours."

Shocked, Dad looked at Holmdahl and said, "Emil, if I had known then what you're telling me now, you'd still be in that jail. I'm not interested in your G..d....money."

Holmdahl responded, "Ben, what difference does it make whether that head is in the hole where it was, or where it is now?"

Dad rose from the table and left, never to see Holmdahl again.

There was a lot of speculation about what happened to the general's head and its whereabouts. Dad said he learned the answer to that question 45 years later, as you will soon learn.

Villa had retired on July 28, 1920, when he signed a document of surrender with the Mexican federal government. Upon his retirement, as noted in an earlier chapter, the government made him a hacendado (landowner) by giving him a 25,000-hectare ranch 80 kilometers southeast of Parral. Along with the ranch, he received an annual stipend of a general's pay, and funds to maintain his ranch, cattle, and retainers. Part of the deal was pay for fifty men who had been his dorados during his revolutionary days. They worked on his ranch and served as bodyguards. In return, Villa agreed to settle down, become a law-abiding citizen, and fight no more.

Unfortunately for him, however, some of his enemies didn't take the peace pledge, for on July 20, 1923, while driving in his 1919 black Dodge roadster in Parral, he and six companions were ambushed by seven men, who shot and killed Villa and five of his

EL PASO HERALD POST
8 February 1926 1:4

ROB VILLA GRAVE

VILLA'S BODY IS ACCUSER IN GRIM CASE

8 February 1926 1:1

American Soldier Of Fortune Jailed Following Grave Robbery.

BANDIT'S HEAD HAS VANISHED

Believe Decapitation Was Made For Sale To Some Institution.

PARRAL, MEXICO, Feb. 8 (AP)—The headless body of Francisco "Pancho" Villa, notorious bandit-rebel chieftain, whose cement sepulchre was torn open by ghouls Friday night, may be the silent accuser of Emil Holmdahl, American soldier of fortune, and a Mexican, Alberto Corral, said to be of Los Angeles.

Holmdahl, reputed to have been a guide for Pershing's fruitless expedition after Villa, and Corral are in jail here while authorities are trying to learn what was done with Villa's head, which the grave robbers cut off and took.

Decapitation Puzzles

No satisfactory explanation has been ascribed for the gruesome decapitation, although a note left with the body said the head was to be sent to Columbus, N. M., scene of the bandit raid in 1916 that resulted in the American punitive expedition.

Many here, however, believe the arch killer's head was filched from the tomb for surreptitious sale to some institution for scientific study. Little is known as yet of the circumstances resulting in the arrest of Holmdahl and Corral. They are said to have maintained they were in this section on a hunting trip.

Solution Wanting

Investigators have taken their lead from a reported inquiry recently by an American as to the exact location of Villa's grave, which was pointed out by the cemetery caretaker.

Conditions about the grave offered small aid to solution of the mystery, except it must have taken a number of strong men to dislodge the weighty concrete covering slab. Liquor bottles and corks smelling of pungent chemicals found near the grave are unaccounted for. The body was left partly exposed to view, apparently having been moved only enough for the decapitators to do their work.

Villa was buried here in 1923, following his death at the hands of some of his disgruntled henchmen.

Bound For Columbus

CHIHUAHUA CITY, Mex., Feb. 8 (AP)—The bandits who broke open the vault containing Gen. Francisco's body and cut off his head are on their way to Columbus, N. M., according to telephone advices received today from the chief of the defensas sociales in Bosque Bonito, Chih.

Troops were dispatched by the commander of the Chihuahua garrison to catch the bandits. They left a note in the grave saying they would deliver Villa's head to Columbus for $5000.

Emil Holmdahl, who is reported under arrest in Parral in connection with the grave desecration, has been interested little in mine development in Chihuahua and was associated with Al Jennings recently in El Paso in one project.

Article in El Paso Herald, February 8, 1926.
Courtesy of Arizona Historical Society

men. Twelve bullets pierced Villa's body, while four shots hit him in the head. The Dodge touring car was also shot full of holes. His last words were reported to be: "Don't let it end like this. Tell them I said something."

Assassinated body of Pancho Villa, over car door.
Courtesy of Center for Big Bend Studies, *The Secret Family of Pancho Villa: An Oral History*, by Rubén Osorio, published 2000

Villa was buried on July 21, 1923, in the Parral cemetery, where his body rested until February 26, 1926, when the cadaver was removed and its head severed, never to be publicly seen again.

The remainder of Villa's body was reburied in Parral, but it did not stay there. In 1976, President Luis Echeverría felt that the proper place for Villa's remains was the Monument of Revolutionary Heroes in Mexico City. On November 18, his remains were solemnly dug up in Parral and taken to the Monument of the Revolution in Mexico City. Thus, 53 years after his death, he received the kind of official recognition and burial he did not obtain when he was assassinated.

What happened to the skull? There have been a number of

stories relating to its disappearance, some imagined, some manufactured, some based on hypothesis, and some just plain guessing.

Alexandra Robbins wrote a comprehensive book titled *Secrets of the Tomb*, which was originally published in September 2002. She speaks of the idiosyncrasies of the Skull and Bones Society, the secret, senior men's group founded at Yale University in 1832. She asserts:

"This society [Skull and Bones] also encourages grave robbing: Deep within the bowels of the tomb are the stolen skulls of the Apache Chief Geronimo, Pancho Villa, and former President Martin Van Buren."

Is that true? What did happen to Villa's skull, and where is it today?

After parting company with the major in El Paso, Dad gave little thought to Villa's skull and Emil Holmdahl until 45 years later. One day in the early 1970s, Dad went to visit an old friend, Frank C. Brophy, at his office in Phoenix.

Into our tale now comes Frank Cullen Brophy,(2) who was born in 1894 in Bisbee, the son of William Henry Brophy. He was one of the powerful movers and shakers in the formation and growth of Arizona from his birth until his death in Phoenix in 1978.

William Brophy prospered, enabling him and his wife, Ellen A. Brophy, to become in later years generous philanthropists. After William Brophy's death, his wife carried on the philanthropy the two had begun. Their contributions to a number of charities led to the founding of Loretto Academy at Douglas and Brophy College Preparatory in Phoenix, which Ellen Brophy built in her husband's memory in 1928. St. Augustine Cathedral at Tucson and the Church of the Blessed Sacrament in Hollywood were recipients of generous support from the Brophy family, as well. All continue to operate to this day.

My father and Frank Cullen Brophy's friendship originated when they were both young men, and continued until Frank's death in 1978.

My grandfather, Marion Williams, had died in Douglas on July 19, 1963. Shortly thereafter, Frank Brophy sent the following letter to Dad:

"I think Marion must have been about the last of the old timers who built up this part of the country and saw the end of the Apache wars and went through the Mexican revolutions. What a group they were---small in number and big in quality....The world seems to be long on success these days and short on men of honor and integrity who won't be pushed around."

Brophy had a keen mind for business and was ever watchful for potential opportunities which might arise. On June 17, 1964, he wrote another letter to Dad in Douglas. The letter said, among other things, that he had learned of a block of land in Puerto Peñasco (Rocky Point) in Sonora, Mexico, that could be acquired. He asked Dad if he would be interested in going into a venture with him to develop and promote the land. He pointed out that, in his opinion, with proper financing and a few of the right kind of people who were familiar with operating in Mexico, "we might be able to do something very worthwhile here."

Brophy went on to say that because of the growing population in Arizona and the attraction of Rocky Point for sports, recreation, and retirement living, it could be a real winner.

How true and accurate Brophy's assessment proved to be; just look at Rocky Point with all of its development today. Dad and Frank continued to be good friends but never became associated in business in the Mexican venture.

Dad mentioned in his 1984 book[37] an occurrence and discussion held in Brophy's office, as follows:

"On one occasion, when I was in Phoenix for a highway department meeting, I stopped by to see an old friend, Frank Brophy. Frank had sold the Bank of Douglas and moved his office from the bank building to his home in Phoenix. He had an office over the garage, with an outside stairway leading up to it. It was very

---

37 *Let the Tail Go with the Hide*

Official Highway Department photo of Ben F. Williams, Sr., when he was a member of the Commission.
Courtesy of Arizona Highway Department (photo #12803-4)

nice, several large rooms, with pictures and plaques on the walls. Among them was a plaque of the Skull and Bones Society. I said, 'I see that you're a member of the Skull and Bones.'"

"Yes, do you know anything about it?"

"Only that I think they had a chapter at Berkeley when I was there," Dad replied.

Brophy continued: "It's an honorary society–a very closed deal. Each class vies with every other class to obtain the skull of a prominent person. We have one of the most famous skulls in the world. We have Pancho Villa's skull in our house at Yale."

"Well, if you have Pancho Villa's skull," Dad commented, "I can tell you how you got it."

Dad's story continued: "He was flabbergasted when I told him about Holmdahl; how I had gotten him out of the Parral jail and about his offer to give me half of the $25,000 he had been paid for taking Villa's head. Brophy said, 'By God, that's right. Five of us put up $5,000 apiece. The other members of Skull and Bones covered his expenses.'"

In an oral history recorded by Lawson Smith and Sherman Hazeltine on March 21, 1982, taken at Dad's office in the Gadsden Hotel in Douglas, Arizona, Dad related essentially the same story that he wrote in his book, with one difference. In the oral history, he referred to the plaque on Frank Brophy's wall as the Skull and Keys. In his book, he called the plaque that of the Skull and Bones.

Forty-five years elapsed between the time my father last saw Emil Holmdahl and Dad's meeting with Frank Brophy in Phoenix in 1971.

Extensive research into this matter reveals that Frank Cullen Brophy was *not* a member of either the Skull and Bones or Skull and Keys when he attended Yale. Rather, my research has revealed that Brophy *was* a member of Pi Tau, Elihu, and another secret society known as "Delta Kappa Epsilon" or "DKE" (the "Dekes"). The DKE society was established June 22, 1844, at Yale University.

In his book, Dad stated, "When asked by Frank, 'Do you know anything about it?' I replied, 'Only that I think they had a chapter at Berkeley when I was there.'"

Research has shown that there was no chapter of Skull and Bones at Berkeley. There was, however, a chapter of Delta Kappa

Epsilon (DKE) when Dad attended college at UC Berkeley.[38]

Frank's statement, "It's an honorary society–a very closed deal" could have referred to a society other than the Skull and Bones.

Many stories have been written about the Skull and Bones tomb and its contents, with some speculation that there are a number of skulls within the tomb, and further speculation that one is the skull of Pancho Villa.

A book written by Antony C. Sutton, *America's Secret Establishment, An Introduction to the Order of Skull and Bones*, published in 2002, lists the names of each group of fifteen members chosen annually. Skull and Bones refers to the list as its "catalog," starting with the first group in 1833 up through the class of 1985. Brophy's name does not appear in any of the rolls of "Bones."

In addition, an e-mail from Nancy Lyon, archivist at Yale University, responding to my inquiry, states:

June 11, 2009
Dear Mr. Williams:

This is in reply to your e-mail inquiry of June 10, 2009, regarding Frank Brophy. My assumption is that you are researching Frank (formerly Francis) Cullen Brophy, Yale Class of 1917.

I consulted the catalogues of the Skull and Bones Society and the Scroll and Key Society from 1915-1925. I did not find Frank Brophy listed as a member of either society.

According to the Class of 1917 classbook, Brophy "won a first colloquy rank; was a participant in the Yale Debating Association, contributed to the (Yale Daily) News and The Hypodermic; and sang in the Freshman Glee Club. He went out for swimming, baseball, and golf, and was on the Water-polo Team in Junior year. He was president of

---

38 Delta Kappa Epsilon's first west coast chapter was founded at the University of California at Berkeley in 1876.

the Yale Catholic Club. He is a member of Pi Tau, Delta Kappa Epsilon, and the Elihu Club.

  If you have any additional questions, please do not hesitate to contact us.

Sincerely,
Nancy F. Lyon
Archivist, Manuscripts and Archives

The *New Yorker*, in an issue dated November 27, 1989, carried a story by Mark Singer, which stated:

It is a simple fact that Frank Brophy graduated from Yale College, but was never a member of Skull and Bones, the most myth-shrouded of Yale's undergraduate senior societies. Whatever hung on Brophy's wall would therefore not have been a plaque of the Skull and Bones Society. This strongly implies, of course, that if Frank Brophy (who died in 1978) told Ben Williams (who died in 1985) that he and four Bones accomplices had paid $25,000 for Pancho Villa's cranium, his object was to embroider an anecdote that sounded to him more colorful than truthful. It also implies that Brophy was the sort of person who would have enjoyed knowing that a casual, innocent prevarication of his could resurface and cause a stir in El Paso many years later. Above all, it implies that Frank Brophy and Ben Williams would have fitted right in with the Wednesday Group in El Paso[39] . . . along the blurry border, where the truth can often become as cloudy as the water in the Rio Grande, where history has immediacy and mythology counts for a lot . . . simple facts tend to ferment a while before they are allowed to imply much at all.

---

39 A group of El Paso's notable and influential movers and shakers which met on Wednesdays.

I believe Mr. Singer's statement that whatever hung on Brophy's wall was not a "plaque of the Skull and Bones Society" is correct. I also believe that, either lost in transcription or translation, the two men (Dad and Brophy) were speaking of a different society, possibly DKE, rather than Skull and Bones.

Having personally known Frank Brophy, I take issue with Singer's statement that "Brophy was the sort of person who would have enjoyed knowing that a casual, innocent prevarication of his could resurface and cause a stir in El Paso many years later." Further, I never knew Dad to prevaricate, even to spice up or embellish a story. From my personal knowledge of Frank Brophy and his family, I sincerely doubt there were any deliberate falsehoods uttered at any time by any of them, and certainly not by Frank Brophy to my father.

A number of other writers have written about the skull's theft and disappearance and have suggested a number of differing scenarios:

Haldeen Braddy wrote an article entitled "The Head of Pancho Villa," which appeared in 1960 in *Western Folklore*, a journal published by Texas Western College. Braddy stated that Emil Holmdahl was a celebrated soldier of fortune who at one time had sided with Villa, and while in Parral was arrested on or about February 6, 1926, and charged with unearthing Villa's corpse and severing its head.

Braddy further states: "A rumor that the gringo Holmdahl stole Villa's head and delivered it to an American scientific institute was widely accepted as fact."

Several other accounts were advanced as to what happened to Villa's head. Some said that a plane had landed on the night of the decapitation carrying an unidentified Mexican general, who took the cranium.

Elias L. Torres, in his work, *La Cabeza de Villa*, 1938, states that the head today rests in Mexico in the control of a noted Mexican official; that Emil Holmdahl delivered the severed head of Villa to the plane in Parral on the night of the theft; and further, that "on the day of his trial, Holmdahl did not have the head in his possession."

Villa's tomb in Parral.
Courtesy of Armando Elías

The *El Paso Herald Post* wrote several stories relative to the disposition of Pancho's skull. A news item dated February 6, 1926, with a dateline from Parral, Chihuahua, says:

> Breaking into the grave of Pancho Villa Friday night, a group of unidentified Mexicans severed the head from the body and paraded the streets with the head on a long pole. The body was replaced in the coffin and the grave covered again. Efforts to locate the grave looters has [sic] proved unavailing up to noon Saturday.

Of course, the part about parading through the streets with Villa's head on a long pole is grossly exaggerated. Had that been done, there would be many people who would know about it.

Another story from the same newspaper, dated February 8, said:

> American Soldier of Fortune Jailed Following Grave Robbery. Bandit's Head Has Vanished. Believed Decapitation Was Made for Sale to Some Institution.
>
> The headless [skeleton?] of Francisco 'Pancho' Villa, notorious bandit-rebel chieftain, whose cement sepulcher was torn open by ghouls Friday night, may be the silent accuser of Emil Holmdahl, American soldier of fortune, and a Mexican, Alberto Corral, said to be of Los Angeles. Holmdahl, reputed to have been a guide for Pershing's fruitless expedition after Villa, and Corral are in jail here while authorities are trying to learn what was done with Villa's head, which the grave robbers cut off and took.

Another story in the *Herald Post* was datelined Chihuahua City, Mexico, February 8:

> The bandits who broke open the vault containing General Francisco's body and cut off the head are on their way to Columbus, N.M., according to telephone advices received today from the chief of the Defensas Sociales in Bosque, Bonito, Chih. Troops were dispatched by the commander of the Chihuahua garrison to catch the bandits. They left a note in the grave saying they would deliver Villa's head to Columbus for $5,000.

The *Herald Post*, on February 9, carried an article entitled, "U.S. Investigates Holmdahl's Arrest." The article stated:

> Washington, D.C., February 9. A.P. The State Department today promised Representative McLeod, Republican, Michigan, to make a thorough investigation of the case of

Emil Holmdahl of Detroit, reported held at Parral, Mexico, in connection with the breaking open of the grave of Gen. Pancho Villa. Mr. McLeod said the department had assured him it would get in touch with the American consul and ask that charges against Holmdahl be thoroughly inquired into. Holmdahl, he said, enlisted in the 16th [sic] United States Engineers in Detroit in 1917.

An article, under dateline February 11, in the *Herald Post*, "Expect Holmdahl to Reach El Paso By Friday Night," states:

Was it the action of Mayor Alberto Almeida of Juarez in getting in quick touch with his brother, Gov. Antonio Almeida of Chihuahua, or intervention of the United States State Department which caused the release of Louis [sic] Holmdahl from Parral prison? The question is unanswered by his friends.

The American consul in Chihuahua was petitioned to investigate and he likely was responsible for state department intervention, it is believed here. Upon receipt of affidavits that Mr. Holmdahl's movements, carefully checked, showed he could not have been in Parral at the time of the ghoul activity, the district attorney in Juarez wired the district attorney in Parral that there was no desire to hold the soldier of fortune. Mr. Holmdahl was a civilian guide to the Pershing punitive expedition into Mexico, giving chase to Villa and his band after the notorious raid on Columbus, N.M.

Another article, dated February 11, dateline Mexico City, reports:

The afternoon paper Grafico prints a story, otherwise completely unsubstantiated here, quoting an anonymous

American just arrived from the north to the effect that the head of Gen. Francisco Villa has been cut off at the instigation of an 'eccentric Chicago millionaire, a student of criminology' who had sent emissaries to Mexico with instructions to get Villa's head at any cost.

Under dateline from Chicago February 12, the same newspaper reports:

> Villa's Head On Its Way To Chicago--Eccentric Windy City Millionaire Financed Grave Robbery---Pathological Examination---Specialist To Study Brain Interest Of Science.
>
> Chicago scientists have admitted that the head of Francisco Villa, described as 'the greatest criminal of the age,' is on its way to Chicago for examination by experts. The disappearance of Villa's head from the bandit chieftain's grave near Parral, Mexico, the night of February 5, was followed by a story in El Grafico of Mexico City that an 'eccentric Chicago millionaire interested in criminology' had financed the theft.
>
> The Chicago millionaire has not been identified, but Dr. Orlando P. Scott, prominent Chicago brain specialist, has announced that he expected the head would arrive here within a few days.

Other speculations were that the head was taken to an airstrip where a waiting airplane flew off with the ghoulish object. Further, some speculate that the skull rests today on the desk of some prominent Mexican who has had it in his possession for many years.

I believe that my father was telling the truth about seeing a plaque on the wall in Frank Brophy's office. I also believe that the two men had a discussion relative to a secret society and the disappearance of Pancho Villa's skull.

I doubt, from everything I've been able to determine from books, articles, magazines, and personal interviews that the skull reposes in the tomb of the Skull and Bones at Yale University. But if not in the Skull and Bones tomb, then where?

I do in fact believe that Holmdahl took the skull, or was directly responsible for its theft. I strongly suspect that Holmdahl made arrangements for the skull to be flown out of Parral on the evening of the theft. Who was the pilot? I don't know.

There are stories of various Mexican generals and former highly placed Mexican politicians who wanted Villa's skull as a keepsake or trophy for their own personal gratification.

The story that the skull wound up in some scientific institution for analysis of Villa's brain to study his uncanny military prowess is hardly credible. I am not a scientist, but I cannot fathom how anybody could analyze a brain to determine what makes a person a military genius. In fact–surely I am right–the brain would long ago have disintegrated.

I suppose in the eighty-plus years since the disappearance of the skull that it could have been disposed of by someone not wanting to become embroiled in any controversial matter relating to it. There are a great number of Mexicans who would dearly like to know that the head will be reunited with the body at its final burial place in Mexico City at the Revolutionary Monument cemetery.

In the past there has been political anxiety created by persons wishing to charge the Bush family–Prescott, George H.W., and George W.– with keeping the skull at the tomb of the Skull and Bones at Yale. The anxiety grew much more intense during the political campaigns and administrations of George H.W. and George W. Bush.

Who has the skull today? I can only speculate, as you the reader can also speculate. But I truly believe that the skull was stolen by Major Holmdahl from Villa's burial site in Parral in 1926, and that it was acquired by some person or persons who paid a considerable amount of money to obtain the cranium.

Where's Pancho's skull today? You tell me.

17

THE SECRET SOCIETIES

Skull and Bones is the secret society that many people believe possesses Pancho Villa's skull in their "tomb" at Yale today. An article by Zack O. Greenberg in the *New Yorker* in January 2004 alleges that the Bush family was instrumental in the original theft of Villa's skull and its subsequent placement in the tomb of the Skull and Bones at Yale. Greenberg's article ("Bones May Have Pancho Villa's Skull") also states that Frank Brophy had purchased Villa's skull for $25,000 from Emil Holmdahl. The article further refers to Alexandra Robbins' book, *Secrets of the Tomb*, which states that Villa's skull rests in the Skull and Bones' "tomb."

In order to get a clearer picture of secret societies, we must examine the beginnings of the college fraternity system. That system in American history began in 1738 at Yale University when a debating society called "Crotonia" and two other societies, "Linonia" (1753), and "Brothers in Unity" (1766), were founded. Shortly thereafter, a chapter of Phi Beta Kappa was also started at Yale, originating from a secret academic society started at the College of William and Mary in 1776.

Later, in 1832, Phi Beta Kappa was converted from a secret academic society into a recognized honor fraternity. It had been, and continues to be, founded upon academic excellence. In 1832, Skull and Bones started at Yale. With the opening of ten residential colleges in 1832 which provided elaborate facilities for good living and dining, the popularity of underclass fraternities began to wane.

Skull and Bones emblem

Skull and Keys is one of the oldest men's honor societies at UC Berkeley. The society was founded at Berkeley in 1892 as an upper classman society for members of Theta Nu Epsilon, which originated in 1881.

Frank Brophy attended Yale in 1917, and my father attended the University of California at Berkeley in 1923. When Dad was a student at UC Berkeley, there was an active chapter of Skull and Keys at the college.

Note the similarity between the emblems of the Skull and Bones and the Skull and Keys.

There was also an active chapter of Delta Kappa Epsilon at UC Berkeley in 1923. DKE began as a secret society at Yale in June of 1844. A chapter of DKE was also chartered at UC Berkeley in 1876. The fraternity recruited men who combined equal proportions of "gentleman, scholar, and jolly good fellow." The DKE society boasts that it was the first college fraternity to erect a "tomb."

Members of DKE have included such notable people as Henry Cabot Lodge, J.P. Morgan, William Randolph Hearst, Theodore Roosevelt, Admiral Robert E. Perry, and Cole Porter. Its mem-

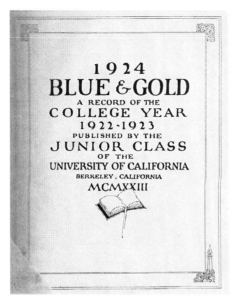

Front page, 1923 Yearbook,
University of California, Berkeley

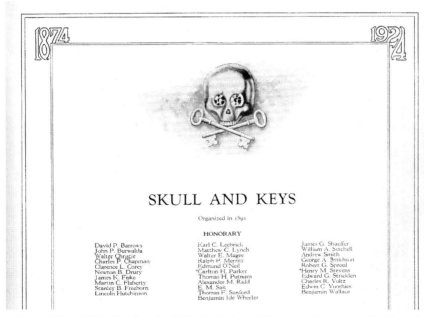

SKULL AND KEYS

Organized in 1892

HONORARY

David P. Barrows
John P. Burwalda
Walter Christie
Charles P. Chapman
Clarence L. Corey
Newton B. Drury
James K. Fiske
Martin C. Flaherty
Stanley B. Freeborn
Lincoln Hutchinson

Karl C. Leebrick
Matthew C. Lynch
Walter E. Magee
Ralph P. Merritt
Edmund O'Neil
Carlton H. Parker
Thomas H. Putnam
Alexander M. Ridd
E. M. Sait
Thomas F. Sanford
Benjamin Ide Wheeler

James G. Shaeffer
William A. Setchell
Andrew Smith
George A. Smithson
Robert G. Sproul
Henry M. Stevens
Edward G. Stricklen
Charles R. Voltz
Edwin C. Voorhies
Benjamin Wallace

Page 369, 1923 Yearbook, UC Berkeley   Note similarity to Skull and
Bones emblem

bership also includes five former U.S. presidents. It now boasts membership of 70,000 men who have become brothers since the fraternity's founding.

Looking at the credentials of DKE at Yale, we find that it owned a tomb which the fraternity built in 1861 and which was maintained until it was sold in 1927.

Now examine the emblems of the societies that Frank Brophy belonged to and compare them to those of the Skull and Bones and the Skull and Keys. Could a quick view of these emblems lead one toward identity confusion? Which emblem did Williams see in Brophy's office?

Reviewing the facts, we find the following:

1. Frank Brophy attended Yale from 1917 through 1921, and while a student there, was a member of Elihu, Delta Kappa Epsilon, and Pi Tau.

2. Elihu and Pi Tau did not have chapters at UC Berkeley when my father, Ben Williams, attended Berkeley.

3. Delta Kappa Epsilon did have chapters at both Yale and UC Berkeley.

4. Skull and Keys had a chapter at UC Berkeley when my father attended there.

5. Pancho Villa was assassinated at Parral, Mexico, on July 20, 1923. His body was interred in the cemetery at Parral.

6. Ben Williams and Emil Holmdahl had maintained a friendship in El Paso, Texas, prior to the date of the removal of Villa's skull.

7. Emil Holmdahl admitted to Ben Williams that he stole Pancho Villa's skull from its place of burial in Parral on February 26, 1926.

8. Frank Brophy admitted that he collaborated in the acquisition of Pancho Villa's skull by contributing $5,000 toward the $25,000 purse that was paid to Emil Holmdahl for stealing the skull.

Skull and Bones tomb at Yale This is where many believe Pancho Villa's skull reposes.

DKE tomb at Yale

Pi Tau
had no
tomb

Elihu building at Yale. Only society whose building has windows, although they are shaded. Building was built on a basement that was constructed in the early 1600s.

DKE emblem

Pi Tau emblem

Elihu emblem

But there are still unanswered questions:

Was Villa's skull deposited in the Skull and Bones tomb, the Delta Kappa Epsilon tomb, or some other tomb at Yale?

Who were the other four men who contributed $5,000 each for the acquisition of Villa's skull?

Where is Villa's skull today?

18

EMIL HOLMDAHL

Emil Lewis Holmdahl was born into a family of Swedish immigrants on August 26, 1883, at Fort Dodge, Iowa. He was tall and matured early. Not satisfied to be a farmer like his family, at age fifteen he enlisted in the U.S. Army. The Spanish-American war was in progress.

He was a true adventurer and soldier of fortune, who later fought in the mountains and jungles of Asia and through the swamps and crumbling ancient cities of Latin America. He participated in many ferocious battles of the Mexican revolution. In August 1913, Holmdahl was a machine-gun commander for Pancho Villa.

In a heated battle at the city of San Andrés, Mexico, Villa's forces were halted by artillery and rifle fire from defending federal general, Felix Terrazas. Unable to proceed further, Villa ordered Holmdahl and his machine guns forward to the firing line to overcome federal troops who were holding up the advance.

In order to defeat his opponents, Villa ordered the execution of his famous *golpe terrifico* (terrific blow), a charge by his elite, well-trained cavalry known as *los dorados* (the golden ones). Turn-

Emil Holmdahl

ing his machine guns over to a subordinate officer, Holmdahl mounted a horse, riding to lead Villa's attacking dorados against Terraza's forces. The charge overwhelmed the defenders. For his bravery and effective leadership, the Mexican government later bestowed upon Holmdahl its legion of honor and made him an honorary colonel in the Mexican army.

For a long time, Holmdahl had wanted to become an officer in the American army. On December 24, 1913, he wrote to the U. S. Adjutant General in Washington, D.C.: "Have just resigned as first captain of artillery with General Pancho Villa's rebel forces in Chihuahua. My reasons for doing such were on account of ill feelings and petty jealousies shown me by my superior officer."

His letter continued: "Can speak the Spanish language fluently. While campaigning through thirteen [Mexican] states, I have learned the water holes and trails.

"Before leaving Villa's forces, have taken a full list of all artillery and small arms."

Previously, Maj. Holmdahl had been a spy, arms agent, and smuggler for the Carranza faction, which was opposing Villa.

In October of 1914, while on a train from Texas to Douglas, Arizona, Holmdahl was arrested and charged with smuggling guns and war materials. As the train pulled into the Douglas depot, officers from the Bureau of Investigation (later the FBI) removed him from the train. After moving a boxcar from the train to a siding, they opened crates in the railcar. Inside were found 100 saddles, bridles, and horse blankets, 75 cases of .30-.30 cartridges, 50 cases of 7-mm. carbine ammunition, 400 canteens, 160 .30-.40 caliber rifles, and 19 boxes of other rifles. Included as well was a box of bugles.

On October 14, 1915, Holmdahl and others went on trial in El Paso's federal district court, charged by the U.S. government with violations of the 1911 neutrality laws which made it a crime to recruit troops for foreign armies on U.S. soil. The conspirators were also charged with attempting to smuggle arms and ammunition across the U.S.-Mexico border at Douglas, a crime as well.

A year later, they were tried. The trial was brief. A number of American and Mexican officers, as well as arms salesmen, testified. The jury was convinced of the guilt of the defendants and agreed on a verdict of guilty of smuggling arms and recruiting fighters to go to Mexico to join in the revolution.

Holmdahl, having been found guilty of recruiting and gun-running, was sentenced by the federal judge to 18 months in a federal penitentiary. No fine was levied, and upon posting a bond of $7,500 pending appeal, he was released from custody.

While his case was being appealed, Holmdahl applied for a commission as an officer in the United States cavalry on December 29, 1915. His application stated that he held the rank of Colonel of Cavalry with the Carranza forces and was formerly chief of artillery under Villa.

He received a letter denying his application. The letter read: "No applicant is eligible for appointment to second lieutenant who is more than thirty years of age." At the time, Holmdahl was thirty-two. The government's reply made no mention of the fact that he was a convicted felon.

Fortunately for Holmdahl, while his appeal was pending, Pancho Villa attacked Columbus, New Mexico. Almost immediately, Gen. John J. Pershing was sent into Mexico as leader of an expeditionary force to chase, capture, and/or kill Pancho Villa. Holmdahl, as an American scout who knew the country well and had previously fought for Villa, enlisted in Pershing's punitive campaign. Although he had been convicted of a felony, his service was accepted by Pershing because of his knowledge of the land, the language, and Villa's military tactics.

Meanwhile, Holmdahl contacted many of his influential friends, asking them to intercede on his behalf to seek a presidential pardon, thereby relieving him of the burden of guilt and prison sentence. Their efforts ultimately resulted in the granting of a full and complete presidential pardon from President Woodrow Wilson on July 13, 1917.(1)

Immediately after the pardon was granted by the President, Holmdahl enlisted as a private in the 6th Engineer Regiment. After giving Holmdahl a physical, Lieutenant H.L. Taylor, a medical corps physician, determined that Holmdahl was unfit for service because of pain and limited flexibility in his right knee, due to shrapnel wounds he had received in 1910.

Holmdahl still had many friends in high places, including not only military officers, but elected officials. When Adjutant General G.W. Read learned of Holmdahl's rejection for military service, he sent a message to the proper authorities stating, "Enlist that man if he only has one leg."

Because of the intervention of higher authority, a memo was put in the adjutant general's files stating that "the Secretary of War authorizes the enlistment of Emil L. Holmdahl in the Sixth Regiment, Engineers, National Army, waiving the defects reported."

Although starting as a private, Holmdahl quickly rose in the ranks to sergeant then to 2nd lieutenant and, in a matter of weeks, to the rank of 1st lieutenant. As a result of his meritorious and valiant service, Holmdahl was promoted to captain on July 30, 1918.

At one time, after his service with the expeditionary force in Mexico, Holmdahl claimed to have been offered $100,000 by a Pershing aide to assassinate Villa. Because of Holmdahl's reputation as a fearless warrior and his knowledge of Villa and his personal life and habits, it was felt that if anybody could kill the man, it was Emil Holmdahl. If the story is indeed true, for some reason he didn't see fit to assassinate the centaur of the north.

In his book, *Soldier of Fortune*, published in 2003, Douglas Meed wrote that in later years Holmdahl made his headquarters at the Sheldon Hotel in El Paso. He describes the hotel as being a rambling, four-story brick building in the center of downtown El Paso, with a reputation as the finest hotel on the border. It featured a gourmet cook and the best-stocked bar in Texas.

Holmdahl gained a reputation as a raconteur of border adventures. The owner of the Sheldon Hotel, Joe Goodell, described Holmdahl as "sporting a black diamond ring on his finger, wearing flamboyant clothes and attracting attention wherever he went." Goodell told of providing the famous mercenary, gunrunner and scout with a free room because of his influence in bringing prospective patrons to the hotel.

Holmdahl died in California on April 8, 1963, while loading his automobile in preparation for a prospecting trip into a remote area of Mexico. He was seventy-nine years of age.

19

THE GENERAL'S SABER

In the 1940s, my father, Ben F. Williams, Sr., was part owner of the Palomas Ranch in Chihuahua, Mexico. The ranch had been purchased by five partners who bought it from a bank in Los Angeles. When the mortgage was paid off, the partners divided the place, with Dad taking two pastures and one-fifth of the cattle and horses as his share. Dad called his new ranch Las Palmas (the palms).

Las Palmas totaled 286,000 acres, upon which Dad built a new ranch house. He also constructed a cowboys' bunkhouse, kitchen, garage, storage room, and a building for a Kohler electric plant. A well was drilled to provide water for the place.

One day, a cowboy brought to the headquarters a saber which he claimed had been taken from the body of a dead Mexican revolutionary general. During the days of the revolution, there were almost as many generals as there were soldiers in the army. On the blade of the saber is impressed "Solengen" and below that "W. Walscheid."

There's no question that the saber and its scabbard came from Mexican revolutionary days. The country was in great turmoil

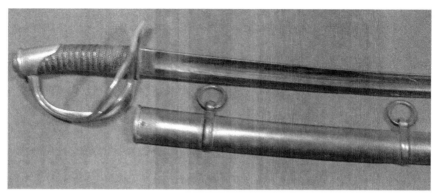

W. Walscheid saber.
Courtesy of Civil War Preservations http://www.civilwarpreservations.com

from 1910 to 1929, with military groups, both government and revolutionary, battling over the land. Many fighting groups crossed the old Palomas Ranch.

I kept the saber and its steel scabbard. They have graced the wall of the den of my home for many years. Recently, I became curious about the saber's origin. I learned that it was made in Germany sometime in the 1850s, and that a great number of such sabers were imported into the United States, where they were used mostly by armies of the North during the U.S. Civil War.

I contacted Kevin Hoffman, owner of Civil War Preservations, an antique weapons dealership in Bethlehem, Pennsylvania. He has several of the Walscheid sabers in his shop. He told me that the swords were imported by the U.S. during the Civil War era, and that it's quite possible that the sword found its way to Mexico and into the hands of a revolutionary general. Many arms, munitions, and military supplies were smuggled into Mexico because of their unavailability in the republic.

If that old saber could only talk to me, I bet it would relate some fascinating tales of Pancho Villa's battles, where it had been, what it had seen and done, and who it had belonged to.

20

VILLA'S LEGACY TO THE PALOMAS

Leaving Nacozari on their way east back to Chihuahua after the Sonoran campaign, the Villistas crossed the Sierra Madre mountains and passed through the old Palomas Ranch. The ranch headquarters was called the "Nogales hacienda,"[40] and a number of Villistas caused destruction to ranch improvements while the main body of Villa's forces proceeded on toward Palomas, Chihuahua, in preparation for their assault on Columbus, New Mexico.

On their way through the Palomas, fences were torn down, and windmills and livestock watering tanks and troughs were destroyed. Great numbers of cattle were unable to water, and died of thirst.

The Palomas Ranch foreman, a man by the name of McKinney, was murdered by Villa's troops.[41] This was by direct order of Pancho Villa. Another American named Corbett was also ordered killed by Villa.

On March 7, 1916, Juan Fondille, an employee of the Palomas, reported to Col. Slocum that some of his men had observed Villa

---

40 The translation of Nogales is "walnuts." Walnut trees were native to certain places on the ranch.
41 See Chapter 12.

and his followers seize four men, among them McKinney and Corbett. When they approached Villa's camp near Casas Grandes, the Americans mistakenly thought the camp was manned by regular Mexican soldiers.

When seized, a Villista colonel, Hernandez, ordered that the Americans be stripped of their clothing and tied to a tree with ropes. The lariats were placed around their necks, and the two Americans were slowly strangled to death. A man and woman being held by the Villistas were able to successfully escape and informed Fondille of the situation.

Predicated upon the killings of its employees and the willful destruction of ranch improvements, a claim was brought by the then owner of the ranch, Henry S. Stephenson, for indemnification against the Mexican government for damages inflicted on the ranch arising out of the Mexican revolution (1910-1915). The claim was presented to and considered by the American-Mexican Claims Commission, which had been established by treaty between the two countries to deal with cases where Americans' property had been taken or destroyed during the Mexican revolution. The program had been instituted to reimburse ranch owners for their losses.(1)

In 1941, the Williams-Greene group[42] bought the Palomas Ranch located in Chihuahua, Mexico. It embraced 2,270,000 acres of land and owned 16,500 head of cattle. During negotiations, the buyers learned that former Mexican president Plutarco Elías Calles (1924-1928) had ordered expropriation of the ranch lands of the Palomas Land and Cattle Company by presidential decree which created a cloud on title.

Possession of the ranch by its former owners, however, was not affected by the decree because the takeover was not enforced until later (1948) by the Mexican government, and then acquisition was accomplished through subterfuge and misrepresentation.

Prior to purchase by the new buyers, a former owner, Henry

---

42 The group consisted of Ben F. Williams, Sr., W.C. Greene, Alfonso Morales, Charles Wiswall, and Al Kalin.

S. Stephenson, had filed a claim for indemnification against the Mexican government for damages to the ranch arising out of the Mexican revolution (1910-1915). It was at the time of purchase of the Palomas from the Security First National Bank of Los Angeles, California, that the Williams-Greene group first learned of the claim of the Palomas owners for damages incurred during the Mexican revolutions. Williams insisted that the claim be withdrawn by the law firm which had filed it for Stephenson, the former owner.(2)

As it ultimately turned out, however, the claim was never withdrawn, and an offer of $1,660,000 was made by the commission to the heirs of Stephenson as indemnification for their losses.

One of the conditions of the law which was passed to indemnify damaged ranch owners was that monetary awards could be made only to American citizens. When the Williams-Greene partnership bought the ranch, it formed a Mexican corporation, as required by the selling bank. The Mexican corporation didn't qualify for the award because it was not an "American citizen."

The Stephenson heirs, as individuals, did qualify, so the money involved in the settlement of the award was held in dispute. Litigation ensued, with a settlement made. The balance of the monies still owing to the Security First National Bank was paid from the settlement proceeds. This satisfied the debt of the Williams-Greene partnership. Attorneys' fees were paid, with some money going to the Stephenson group, and a small balance to the Williams-Greene partners.

When payment of the claim for reimbursement was made, the Mexican government, under then President Miguel Alemán, took the position that the ranch had been "bought" by the government. No mention of reimbursement for revolutionary damages was made. By this time, Ben Williams and his partners had dissolved their partnership. For his part, Williams received the Buena Vista pasture, along with the south part of the "Los Moscos" pasture, both together totaling 286,000 acres. Twenty percent of all cattle and other personal property of the Palomas Company was also transferred to Williams as his share of the assets.

Note civilian post-war Jeep.

Carlos Serrano, president of the Mexican senate, claiming to act on behalf of the Mexican government, flew to Las Palmas (Williams' new ranch) in President Aleman's DC-3. He was accompanied by two Mexican *pistoleros* (bodyguards). They landed on the airstrip which I had built, two miles east of the Las Palmas headquarters.

Dad, Tom Ferrel (his ranch manager), and two Las Palmas *vaqueros* (cowboys) met the President's plane at the strip. Serrano confronted Williams, demanding that he remove his cattle – 8,000 head of steers – and that he vacate the ranch. Williams was given six weeks to accomplish this.

Prior to the encounter with Serrano, Dad had been faced with the closure of the U.S. border by an embargo against the importation of Mexican cattle imposed by the United States. The embargo was ordered on December 27, 1946, after an outbreak of foot-and-mouth disease was reported in southern Mexico. Some "infected" bulls were brought into Mexico at Vera Cruz – their place of origin was Brazil. A few of the infected bulls found their way into Texas, precipitating the border's closing.

With the border closed, and no U.S. market for Mexican cattle, canneries were built along the border to kill and process cattle which could no longer cross as live animals into the United States. One processing plant was under construction in Juarez, across the border from El Paso.

Dad refused to move his cattle or surrender the ranch. It was only through the intervention of my father's politically powerful friends in Mexico that he was able to forestall his eviction until the Juarez cannery was completed and could accommodate his needs.

He delivered 8,000 steers for slaughter to the Juarez cannery, receiving only four and one-half cents per pound for the animals. Prior to the imposition of the quarantine, he had contracted to sell all of his cattle to American buyers for thirty-three cents per pound.

After the cattle had gone to the cannery, Dad abandoned his Las Palmas Ranch, including its fine house and all other improvements.

I don't know who has the ranch today, and frankly, I don't care. What's that saying about crying over spilt milk?

Statue of Pancho Villa in Veinte de Agosto Park, Tucson, Arizona.
Taken by author

21

PANCHO VILLA RIDES AGAIN

Pancho Villa's legend lives on in the southwest and in Mexico. Today, a bronze statue of Villa mounted on a rearing horse[43] stands in the Veinte de Agosto Park in Tucson, Arizona (Veinte de Agosto means 20th of August. It is Tucson's birthday.). The park is in downtown Tucson, between Broadway and Congress Streets, just west of Church Avenue. The statue was a gift to the people of Arizona from the Mexican government and a media organization.

Both Mayor Lewis Murphy and City Councilman Roy Laos opposed the placement of the statue in the Tucson Park.

Murphy was a capable and respected mayor.[44] He didn't want to honor Pancho Villa, who was responsible for the murder of American citizens and the destruction of property in the U.S. Murphy refused to glorify Villa by accepting his bronze image for display in a Tucson city park. The statue eventually was installed in 1981 through the efforts of Governor Bruce Babbitt, who "encouraged its location in Tucson." Mayor Murphy did not

---

43 The statue is 14 feet high and weighs 5 tons. It reputedly cost $260,000.
44 Lew Murphy was mayor of Tucson for sixteen years. I was mayor of Douglas for eight years (1980-1988) during Murphy's term of office. Lew and I became friends.

want to participate in the statue's dedication ceremonies. Both the *Arizona Daily Star* and the *Tucson Citizen* reported on June 26, 1981, that Mayor Murphy "will be unavailable to attend the unveiling ceremony under any circumstances."

There is also a statue of Villa in El Paso, Texas, and reportedly another one in New Mexico, where Villa's deadly attack on the United States at Columbus occurred.

During the days of the Mexican Revolution of 1916, the U.S. government stationed thousands of U.S. soldiers along the border. This was done to prevent the intrusion of aliens into the United States.

The barrier consisted of a large force of armed soldiers placed at strategic places along the border, three thousand infantry and cavalry troopers in trenches at Douglas alone. They were reinforced by well-positioned artillery pieces on surrounding hillsides, where they could see and accurately fire on Agua Prieta and its environs.

To the east, at the San Bernardino Ranch, trained soldiers patrolled both east and west from their base camp. Farther to the east were armed and trained U.S. fighters at Camp Furlong in Columbus, New Mexico. Yet farther east was a large complement of armed troopers at Fort Bliss in El Paso.

To the west of Douglas was a military complement at Camp Newell outside of Bisbee. Fort Huachuca was a large Army post where the Tenth Cavalry and other units were based. Nogales was guarded by troops from Camp Stephen Little.

I grew up in Douglas, Arizona, immediately adjacent to Agua Prieta, Sonora, Mexico. I spent most of my life in Douglas. My grandfather, Marion L. Williams, bought the San Bernardino Ranch from John H. Slaughter's widow, Viola, in 1937. At that time, there was not much of a fence separating the U.S. and Mexico. The fence consisted of a few strands of barbed wire stretched between fence posts. A person could easily pass through, as I did on numerous occasions as a boy when hunting rabbits

American soldier standing at U.S.–Mexico border; Mexican officer mounted on horseback in Mexico.
Courtesy of Bisbee Mining & Historical Museum

Border fence as it looks today, 17 miles east of San Bernardino Ranch, July 2010.
Courtesy of Susie Krentz

or exploring the neighboring ranch to the south. In some places, there was not even wire. At the time of the revolutions, in some places there was no fence at all.

History has a way of repeating itself. Today, the United States is again facing immigration issues at its border with Mexico. And the Mexican government is fighting a large-scale war within its own boundaries—a war against militant, armed, vicious bandits and drug cartel members seeking control of drug distribution in Mexico and the United States.

Pancho Villa rode into the history of the Williams family in Mexican revolutionary days. If he were to ride into our lives today, what part would he play?

Although Villa's image is cast in bronze, does his spirit still linger?

ENDNOTES

CHAPTER 1

(1) My uncle, Dell Williams, bought the Cajon Bonito (Pretty Box) Ranch in Sonora in the early 1940s from the Gabilondo family. Its brand was the Flying X. The ranch was only a few miles from Slaughter's San Bernardino Ranch.

(2) Alfred Paul was the grandfather of Cornelia Paul Kazal, who currently resides with her husband, Albert Kazal, Jr., in Tucson.

(3) The following article appeared in the *Douglas Daily International* on September 1, 1914:
"NEWS OF DOUGLAS
Dr. Alexander V. Bye of Phelps Dodge & Company's Bisbee office came down last night on business and while here attended the reception at the country club [for] Generals Villa and Obregón."

CHAPTER 2

(1) In an oral interview Dr. Osorio conducted with Esperanza Velasquez Bringas at the family's ranch, Dr. Osorio was told that Pancho Villa confided the following information to Velasquez:
"A few years ago, while still fighting in the revolution, in one of my various visits to the city of Parral, I met the elderly owner of a small shop. He had known my mother since she was very young and had also met my paternal grandfather, whose last name was Arango. According to what he told me, my birth father's last name was Fermán. I do not know the reason why my mother

used Villa as her last name. Perhaps it was to keep me away from my father because they never lived together, and she feared that he would take me away from her. The truth is that I grew up as a Villa, and when I learned that my last name was Fermán, it was too late to change it. In my hometown, either nobody knew this story or nobody wanted to tell me about it. Had I been told then, believe me when I say that I would have used my father's last name because, even though I never met my father, I have no hard feelings for him. So my children and I are Fermáns."

(2) At least one person interviewed by Osorio related that when Pancho Villa was born, Augustín Arango was already married to Micaela and that's why they gave the child the name of Arango. Just before she died, the interviewee said, Villa's mother told Villa who his real father was. It was reported that when Doroteo Arango was a child, the sons of rich *hacendados* who lived in San Juan del Rio called him all sorts of names when he accompanied his father, Augustín, to town. Young Doroteo fought them all, returning insults while using his fists or throwing rocks. An older observer stated that Doroteo was an impulsive person, in addition to being a brawler. Through necessity and by nature, he would not let himself be insulted by anyone for any reason. As a teenager, it is reported, Villa was a card shark accustomed to winning money and other items from those who worked the farms along with him.

(3) One official document stated that Augustín Arango and Micaela Arámbula were married in 1877 in the Church of San Fermín de Pánuco, Durango.

(4) Parochial Archive of San Francisco de Asís, San Juan del Rio, Durango, Baptismal Certificate number 223 states: "In the Church of San Juan del Rio, on the seventh day of July, 1878, I, Priest José Andres Palomo, priest in charge of this villa, solemnly baptized a child that was born in Rio Grande, the fifth of last

month. I gave him the name of José Doroteo. He is the legitimate son of Augustin Arango and Micaela Arámbula."

(5) From a book by Rubén Osorio, *The Secret Family of Pancho Villa: An Oral History*:

From a memoir of Lucy Read, who was born in Chihuahua in 1906 of a Mexican mother and English father:

"One morning in February of 1916 when father was away from home, Pancho Villa and some of his troops appeared at our home in Chihuahua, demanding to know the whereabouts of father. Mother answered to Villa that father was in Sonora. All the time his men were ransacking our home and taking our belongings, such as bedding, cooking utensils, jewelry and other property.

"Villa and his men looked for father, but we told them that he was in Sonora. My fifteen-year-old elder brother, George, disguised himself as an old lady dressed in some of mother's clothing. He escaped through the back garden where no guards had been posted and then ran to seek help.

"I was crying for fear of what he [Villa] would do to us and kept hanging onto mother's skirt. Just then, Villa reached out to me and pulled my hair. I still recall his very words: 'Now, *guerita* [fair one], you never see your gringo daddy anymore.' Villa grabbed mother and threw her to the floor, where she fainted. I ran to one of the guards asking for a glass of water for mother, but his reply was, 'I'm sorry. Don't get too close to me, and don't let my general see you talking to me because he will kill us both.'

"A guard came over and told another guard, 'General wants you to pour the oil [coal oil] on the family so we can burn them alive.' The other fellow said, 'Oh, no, I just can't do that, what about the poor children?' The reply was, 'General said, the whole family.'

"Within minutes some of Villa's men arrived with two wagonloads of coal oil to carry out his instructions. Soon Villa's soldiers were running back and forth opening cans of coal oil and pouring it over our home and furniture. Just as they were ready to pour the oil on us, we heard the roar of cannon fire. At this interruption, Villa's soldiers made a run for their horses which were tied to the trees surrounding our house. They left our belongings scattered all over the place because they had no time to take them. One of Villa's men walked toward us with a gun in his hand and with threatening tone said, 'You will escape from being killed this time, but remember, next time, you will all be killed.'"

Lucy Read went on to relate how her family, being the only foreigners in town outside of Casas Grandes, "General Pershing and father became good friends. The general and members of the Red Cross officers would frequently stay in our home to the point that after several weeks we began to feel that they were part of our family. General Pershing took a liking to me since I was about the same age as one of his daughters. [Note: Pershing's three daughters perished in a tragic fire at the Presidio in San Francisco.] He would sit me on his lap and tell me that I looked a lot like one of his little girls, who at that time was living in San Francisco, California, with the rest of his family.

"General Pershing advised father that he should leave and take his family to the United States. We travelled with some of Pershing's troops back to Columbus, and from there went to old Macia [Mesilla] where father acquired a large farm which became our home. We later learned that Villa had burned our home to the ground and destroyed our herd of cattle so that there was nothing for us to go back to Mexico for."

(6) Interview with Art Gaona, by Ben F. Williams, Jr.

I met Art Gaona on April 3, 2010, at his niece's home in Phoenix.

Art's father, Nicholas Gaona, was born in Santa Rosalia, Chihuahua, in 1882. Nicholas was a descendant of Spanish origin whose ancestors came from Spain to Chihuahua decades before. The Gaona family owned lands near Chihuahua City by reason of a Spanish land grant conferred by the king and queen of Spain in the 1700s.

Nicholas Gaona owned a pistol and was acclaimed in his village as an outstanding marksman. Legend had it that on one occasion, when out in the country, he was urged by companions to take a shot at a jackrabbit a long distance away. Drawing his pistol, he fired, killing the rabbit. His fame as a marksman grew as it was passed from mouth to mouth by the people of Santa Rosalia. Villagers acclaimed him to be the best shot in the region.

During revolutionary days, Nicholas Gaona hid his pistol for fear of losing it. He could also be punished and maybe shot by Pancho Villa for concealing the weapon. The legend led Villista troops to believe that Nicholas owned a pistol. They questioned him, but without success. The Villistas also conducted many intense searches of his home and property, but never found the gun. He had hidden it well.

One of the strategies upon which Pancho Villa built his fame and following was by taking land from *hacendados* (land owners) and distributing it among the poor. The Gaona family, identified as Spanish rather than Mexican, was a prime target for such confiscation. Villistas expropriated the Gaonas' lands and distributed them to poor Villista followers.

Because of the harsh treatment they received, Nicholas and his family left Mexico and immigrated to Miami, Arizona. It was in Miami that Art Gaona was born on March 24, 1919.

With the passage of time, the family moved from Miami to Mesa, where Art entered public school at age six. Although he had been placed in kindergarten in Miami, upon reaching Mesa, his teacher brought to the attention of the school principal that Art was a good student who was achieving above the level of kindergarten. Art's principal directed the teacher to advance the boy to first grade. Art graduated from Mesa High School. After graduation, he farmed in the Salt River Valley, then worked in a sheet metal shop after serving in the U.S. Air Force during World War II. He had served in Rome for three years as a noncommissioned communications officer (radio and teletype) specialist. Art's four brothers also entered the U.S. armed forces and served honorably.

He retired after a career working for the Veterans Administration in Phoenix. Art now resides in Phoenix with two unmarried sons.

I found Art a fascinating and articulate man who is fluent in English, Spanish, and Italian. He expressed no interest in going to the family's old home in Santa Rosalia, Chihuahua, where his forebears lived and farmed for many years.

(7) Oscar J. Martinez, in his book, *Fragments of the Mexican Revolution, Personal Accounts from the Border*, relates how the execution of prisoners by firing squad or hanging party organized on the spot was commonplace. So was the unceremonious burning and mass burial of corpses in large, common graves. Martinez relates that the number of Mexicans, including civilians, who died during the revolutionary period was, according to knowledgeable sources, around two million. Among the estimated two million dead were those who perished from malnutrition, disease, and other hardships.

CHAPTER 3

(1) When Granddad was ranching in Sonora during the time of Plutarco Elías Calles' presidency in 1926, he had already established a well-known reputation as a man of great moral courage. He told of one incident during the days of uncertainty and turmoil when he was ranching on the Santa Rosa Ranch in Sonora. At that time, a man named Canuto was *jefe de cordado* (chief of the rural state police), headquartered in Moctezuma several miles from Granddad's ranch. Canuto and his *rurales* had camped at Granddad's ranch and spent the night on a number of occasions.

One evening, he and his company of rurales rode up to the

Santa Rosa, and he spoke to Granddad. He said, "I have a telegram from Calles. I am instructed to go over and get your neighbor, Jesús Elías, and hang him."

He showed Granddad the wire and said, "I know that Jesús is a friend of yours, and he is a good man. I don't want to do this, but I have orders to follow, and I'm going to his ranch tomorrow and carry out the order. I just wanted to let you know about it."

That night after dark, Granddad saddled his horse and rode twenty miles to Arispe, where Jesús Elías lived. He knocked on the door, woke him up, and told him about the telegram Canuto had shown him. He further advised Jesús that he'd better get out of the country.

That night, Jesús rode his horse out of Mexico into Arizona, and escaped the order for his execution.

(2) Linda B. Hall and Don M. Coerver, in their book, *Revolution on the Border*, wrote:

"Besides banditry and revolutionary problems, social disorganization in the camps had caused great difficulties. In 1916 at Cananea, for example, the governor of the state found it necessary to decree the death penalty for ordinary robbery. Lest his warning go unheeded, he ordered the military commander of the town to go ahead and carry out the penalty in the first two or three cases that came up.

"During the revolutionary decade, Mexicans flooded north across the border into the relative safety and stability of the United States. This population movement, which has continued to the present date, has permanent consequences, setting the future patterns that such migrations would follow by establishing large Mexican communities that served as support networks for newcomers . . . .The devastation, chaos, danger, and economic disaster during the period from 1910 to 1920 led to the widespread migration to the safety, if not necessarily comfort, of the United States. Mexicans by the thousands came across the border as legal immigrants, 'temporary' workers, refugees, or illegal aliens.

"In addition to the migrants, permanent or temporary, thousands of refugees were pouring across the border in response to war conditions in northern Mexico. It was not unusual for an entire town to cross the border en masse, either before or during military clashes in the area.

"A somewhat more bizarre group of refugees followed General Pershing's troops out of Mexico in 1917. These were the civilians who had been employed by the U.S. military during Pershing's expedition into Mexico in search of Pancho Villa. They numbered 2,755, of whom 197 were North Americans, 2,030 Mexicans, and 528 Chinese. They all feared reprisals at the hands of angry Mexicans who viewed them as collaborators."

CHAPTER 10

(1) My father maintained a residence in Nacozari in the 1950s to support Mexican immigration requirements in order to permit him to engage in business in Mexico. He owned and operated a copper and molybdenum ("molly") mine southeast of Nacozari, which employed 80 men. From the mine, he shipped three carloads of copper concentrates per month to the Phelps Dodge smelter in Douglas. Moly concentrates from the operation were shipped directly to steel mills in Japan. The steel mills threw the canvas bags of moly in with the molten steel as a hardening agent. Dad also owned a one-quarter interest in the Nacozari Hotel.

(2) That same home is now a museum (the Douglas-Williams House Museum). It serves as headquarters for the Douglas Historical Society, as well as the Cochise County Historical Society and the Douglas High School Alumni Association.

(3) Armando Elías, a longtime and good friend of the author, has written two books, *Compendio de Datos Historicos de la Familiar Elías* (Compendium of the Historical Data of the Elías Family), and *Familia Elías, the Elías Family*.

He is a member of the famous and illustrious Elías family of northern Mexico (principally Sonora) and southern Arizona. Armando said he is a nephew of Plutarco Elías Calles, who was the commanding officer of the federal forces which defeated Villa in early November of 1915 at Agua Prieta (and went on to become Governor of Sonora and President of Mexico). Armando is a former president of the Arizona Historical Society. Many of the photographs and sketches of Calles were generously made available to me by Armando. Some have never before been published.

(4) The source of the information about the four burial markers in the middle of the street is a telephone conversation with José Castellanes, owner of La Azteca Curio Store in Agua Prieta, on November 22, 2009. The Castellanes family has resided in, and conducted business in, Agua Prieta for many years. José has been a source of information for several stories I have written.

CHAPTER 12

(1) Until then, Villa had maintained friendlier relations with the United States than Carranza. Gen. Hugh L. Scott, U.S. Army Chief of Staff, who at one time viewed Villa's dorados on exhibition as a cavalry unit, stated in his memoirs:

"The recognition of Carranza had the effect of solidifying the power of the man who rewarded us with kicks on every occasion, and of making an outlaw of the man who helped us. We permitted Carranza to send his troops through United States soil, by rail, to crush Villa . . . after Villa had given up millions of dollars at the request of the State Department, expressed through me. I have never been put in such a position in my life."

CHAPTER 13

(1) When my cousin Tooter and I were boys of 11 and 12 years of age, we scouted and tramped over almost every square inch of the San Bernardino, and particularly the mesa which had been the military outpost during revolutionary days.

We found brass buttons and emblems from military uniforms, metal stays for ropes used to tie down tents, buckles from harness and cavalry tack, also many rectangular metal feed containers used to feed cavalry livestock. One time, we ran across 40 to 50 spent .30-06 rifle shell cases from what obviously had been a machine gun emplacement, most probably used for training.

CHAPTER 14

(1) In 1891, Pershing was ranked as the second best pistol and fifth best rifle shot in the entire U.S. Army. The 10th Cavalry (Buffalo Soldiers) was formed on September 21, 1866, at Fort Leavenworth, Kansas. In 1895, Pershing was assigned to the 10th Cavalry, where he served from October 1895 to May 1897. It was from his service with the 10th Cavalry black troopers that he was given the name of "Blackjack."

Pershing commanded the United States expeditionary forces in Europe during World War I. He was promoted to the rank of four-star general. On returning to the States after the war, he was offered a promotion to five-star general. He refused, saying he would rather wear four gold stars, which no other general was permitted to wear. At the time, he was the highest ranking general in the U.S. Army, having been promoted, in addition to receiving his gold stars, to the position of General of the Armies.

While serving in Europe during World War I, Pershing established the military police corps (MPs).

Pershing and his sister visited Tucson in 1938, staying at the El Conquistador Hotel, where he became ill. He was hospitalized at the Desert Sanatorium of the Southwest, later to become Tucson Medical Center. Seventy-eight years of age at the time, he was diagnosed with heart trouble. His illness was so critical that his attending doctors advised family members to make arrangements for his funeral. The uniform in which he had said he wanted to be buried was sent for. It was at his home in Kansas. A special railcar was dispatched to Tucson to bear his body to its final resting place for final services and burial. Tucson flower shops loaded their inventories with fresh flowers, expecting a large funeral for the general. They had to dispose of their flowers, however, because the general's condition improved to the point that he left Tucson and lived for another ten years. He died at Walter Reed Hospital on July 15, 1948.

(2) Linda B. Hall and Don M. Coerver, in their book, *Revolution on the Border*, wrote: "The punitive expedition was quite large; organized as a provisional division, it originally consisted of more than 5,000 troops and reached a peak strength of more than 11,000. Further, it penetrated into Mexico more than 300 miles, with the expedition lasting for almost a year."

(3) Patton began his military career at Virginia Military Institute. After one year, he transferred to the United States Military Academy at West Point. Because of poor grades in mathematics, he had to repeat his "plebe" year. Thereafter, he excelled and was appointed cadet adjutant, the second highest position a cadet could achieve. He graduated in 1909 from the Point, receiving a

commission as second lieutenant of cavalry.

Patton participated in swimming events in the 1912 Summer Olympics in Stockholm, where he performed well. He also excelled in pistol shooting, and took great pride in becoming a "master" in the use of the saber. Following the Olympics, Patton studied in Germany under the tutelage of a French master of arms, who taught him fencing. Patton became the youngest-ever "master of the sword" at the Mounted Service School at Fort Riley, Kansas. While there, he designed a new saber for use by both mounted and foot soldiers.

CHAPTER 15

(1) From the book, *Wings Over the Mexican Border*, by Kenneth Baxter Ragsdale:

"The United States Army established an aeronautical division in the Signal Corps on August 1, 1907, acquired the first airplane in 1909, and formed the First Aero Squadron in Texas on March 5, 1913.

"Very strict requirements were set for candidates to become flyers. To be accepted for pilot training: 'The candidate should be naturally athletic and have a reputation for reliability, punctuality and honesty. He should have a cool head in emergencies, good eye for distance, keen ear for familiar sounds, steady head and sound body, with plenty of reserves; he should be quick-witted, highly intelligent and tractable.'

"The First Aero Squadron's departure with the Pershing punitive expedition into Mexico in March 1916 marks the initial use of aircraft by the United States Army in a military operation. The undistinguished record of the fragile Curtiss JN-3 biplanes, used primarily for reconnaissance and carrying dispatches, achieved little to portend the airplane's military potential."

CHAPTER 16

(1) Article 19 of the Mexican Constitution of 1917 states:

"Article XIX–No imprisonment shall exceed the limit of three days without justification or the formal indictment of imprisonment, in which will be expressed the following: the specific crime imputed to the accused, the elements that constitute the same, the place, time and circumstances of execution of the same, and the facts which give rise to the previous, all of which shall be in a form necessary to comprise the corpus of the crime and give rise to probable cause against the accused. Any infraction of this requirement will hold responsible any authority that orders a detention or consents to the same, its agents, ministers, mayors or jailers that execute the same."

(English translation courtesy of Stefano D. "Steve" Corradini)

(2) The Brophy family originated in Ireland, from whence William Henry Brophy migrated to San Francisco in 1881. Unable to find a job in San Francisco, he traveled to Bisbee, Arizona, where he joined his brother, Jim. He punched cows in the Sulphur Springs valley for some time before becoming associated with the Copper Queen Mercantile Company, which was later to become Phelps Dodge Mercantile Company. He was the first manager of the company, having been put in that position by Professor James Douglas, one of the founders of Phelps Dodge Mining Corporation. Freeport McMoRan Copper and Gold Company recently purchased PD which today is the largest publicly traded copper producer in the world.

Many miners and cowboys, needing a place to keep their money, left it on deposit with Billie Brophy in a safe at his store in Bisbee. By this arrangement, Brophy became a one-man bank, which led to the establishment of the Bank of Bisbee in 1900. He and James Douglas then founded the Bank of Douglas, which later evolved to become the Arizona Bank. James Douglas was president, and Billie vice-president. Over the years, their association apparently became onerous, to the point that the two parted ways, with Brophy acquiring Douglas' interest in the bank.

It was during the labor riots at Cananea, Sonora, in 1906 that Col. William C. Greene telephoned Bill Brophy at Bisbee, urgently asking for arms and ammunition to arm Americans who were fearful for their lives at the hands of striking and rioting Mexican workers and sympathizers. Brophy turned over all the weapons and ammunition he had in his Bisbee store to assist in the defense of the Americans in Cananea.

In 1935, the Brophys acquired the Babacomari cattle ranch located north and a little west of Fort Huachuca. Today it belongs to the Brophy Corporation, which continues to operate it.

CHAPTER 18

(1) The following documents are from the records of the Bureau of Investigation (to become the FBI in 1935).

"This is part of a confidential report from Special Agent E.B. Stone to Special Agent Herbert L. Barnes, Special Agent in Charge, Bureau of Investigation, San Antonio, Texas:

"In re Emil L. Holmdahl, Application for Executive Clemency, letter dated February 19, 1917, addressed to Robert L. Barnes, San Antonio, Texas:

"Interviewed Mayor Tom Lea. He states that he does not have a personal acquaintance with Holmdahl, but his information is that Holmdahl has always been very frank in dealing with the authorities at El Paso; that while his reputation was that of a soldier of fortune, yet the Mayor believes that he has always helped the American government and furnished such information from time to time as would be of value to them.

"Interviewed Police Captain Hall . . . . At that time, Captain Hall was in charge of the Secret Service working along the border for Madero, and he states that it is a fact that Holmdahl was employed by him as a secret service man; that he was not discharged and was not looked upon as a double crosser, but to the contrary, he considered him very faithful and valuable . . . . Captain Hall states that when Villa was in control in 1913 and 1914, across the river, that Holmdahl was detailed to sort out a lot of 7 m/m ammunition that had been purchased on this side of the river [Rio Grande] and select the good from the bad; this ammunition had been purchased for Villa by Summerfield; that later, when this ammunition was being used by the Villa forces, it developed that a lot of it was bad; therefore, Holmdahl, having been the man detailed to sort it out, with a lot of Mexicans under him, he was made the goat in the affair and incurred the extreme displeasure of Villa. Capt. Hall states that it is a fact that Holmdahl did accompany Gen. Hill to Veracruz as a captain and later accompanied the Carranzista forces from that point when they captured Mexico City in 1914. Capt. Hall also states that he only knows of the occasions in which Holmdahl was put in jail, the first being the time mentioned when he was jailed by Maytorena in Hermosillo and the second time when he was arrested and put in jail at El Paso by the government for violation of the neutrality laws. Further, that Holmdahl assisted him (Captain Hall), in the matter of obtaining evidence against counterfeiters of Mexican currency and that his efforts in that connection with [were?] on behalf of the government and of great value."

The following is from a Memorandum for the Pardon Attorney, dated March 22, 1917:

"A man very close to the Carranza faction in San Antonio, who wishes his name withheld because of fear of bodily harm, should Holmdahl learn that he is furnishing information, but whose name I will be glad to give you personally, stated that Holmdahl at one time claims to be a German citizen and at the next a Mexican citizen; that he is one of the most troublesome adventurers on the border; that together with a lot of tramps he first served in Garibaldi's foreign legion, during the Madero attack against Navarro at Juarez; that Holmdahl served as a secret service man for the Madero government, but was soon discharged for double dealing; that he afterwards went to work for Diebold, the Huerta counsel at El Paso, after the assassination of Madero (Diebold was indicted for recruiting men at El Paso); that Holmdahl, went to Juarez one night disguised and was captured by the Villistas and would have faced a firing squad but for the intervention of Felix Summerfield, a German, who was one of Villa's advisers, and who claimed that Holmdahl had given him some information about Diebold; that during the Orozco revolution, Holmdahl was mixed up with José Inez Salazar; that these parties together with Ochoa extorted money from Mexicans under a pretext that Salazar, who controlled the territory around Palomas, would destroy windmills and cut range fences; that Holmdahl served with Villa but left after the battle of Torreón, because a lot of worthless ammunition appeared which it was claimed by Villa that Holmdahl and Summerfield had sold him; that Holmdahl was afterwards sent to Sonora by Lazaro de la Garza, the Villa consul at Juarez, to spy on Maytorena and was arrested by Maytorena; that it then appeared that Holmdahl was on the payroll of both the Villistas and Carranzistas; that Maytorena 30-3d [deported] him from Mexican territory and after the Villa break, Holmdahl enlisted with the Carranza forces defending Naco; that for a while he held a commission as lieutenant in the Carranza army under General Benjamin Hill; that Holmdahl accompanied Hill to Veracruz, but soon after appeared in El Paso, mixed up with Ochoa and José Orozco, a brother of the famous bandit, Pasqual Orozco, who was killed by a Texas ranchman in one of his horse stealing forays across the Texas border; that Holmdahl had been in jail many times; that he had been mixed up in all kinds of questionable transactions such as selling bricks for cartridges, selling bad cartridges and gunrunning across the border; that he also was mixed up with a lot of counterfeiters in selling counterfeit Mexican bills; that he is totally unreliable although of pleasing appearance and suave in his manners; that he is one of the most dangerous adventurers on the border."

The following is from a telegram from Special Agent H.L. Barnes to Bielaski, Department of Justice, Washington, dated March 24, 1917, re *United States vs. E. Holmdahl*:

"Telegram received Beldon does not desire his name used concerning Holmdahl matter says is afraid will kill him when released. Chas Stevens claims have similar information to Beldon. Am endeavoring get touch with him and arrange interview. Will wire results. [signed] Barnes."

CHAPTER 20

(1) From the front page of the *Douglas Daily International*, May 8, 1914, dateline El Paso, Texas:

"CHIHUAHUA BANDIT MAKES DEMAND FOR MONEY

Unless three large cattle companies operating in northern Chihuahua pay large sums of money to General Rodrigo Quevedo within twenty-four hours, he will destroy the windmills on the ranches owned by the companies. It is estimated that the loss to the companies should the windmills be destroyed would be more than $1,000,000 within a week as thousands of cattle certainly would die of thirst. The letter from Quevedo demanded that the Palomas Land and Cattle Company pay $5,000 gold, that the San Pedro Cattle Company pay $1,000, and that the Corralitos Cattle Company produce $3,333. He demanded that the money be left at a hacienda near Nogales, Arizona.

Whatever the answer made to the present demand, it is certain that presentations of the strongest kind will be made to General Carranza and General Villa and that they will be asked to send a force which will capture or destroy Quevedo's band or sweep into the arms of the United States troops at the border."

(2) In his book, *Let the Tail Go with the Hide*, at page 144, Ben Williams, Sr., wrote:

"Stephenson had placed a claim against the Mexican government, through the United States State Department, for $4,000,000, which represented damages.

The claim was filed with the American-Mexican Claims Commission, which had been established to deal with claims made by Americans whose property had been taken over or destroyed or who had other suffered a monetary loss as a result of the Revolution.

We signed the contract and agreement for the purchase of the Palomas Ranch February 21, 1941.

This Contract and Agreement made and entered into this 21st day of February, 1941, by and between the PALOMAS LAND AND CATTLE COMPANY, a California corporation, having its principal office and place of business in Los Angeles, California, and the HUECO CATTLE COMPANY, a Texas corporation, having its principal office and place of business in El Paso, Texas, hereinafter called First Parties, and CHARLES E. WISWALL and W. C. GREENE, both residing at Cananea, Sonora, Mexico, A. J. KALIN, residing at Browley, Imperial County, California, and BEN F. WILLIAMS, residing in Cochise County, Arizona, all citizens of the United States, and ALFONSO MORALES, a citizen of the Republic of Mexico but residing in Cochise County, Arizona, hereinafter called Second Parties:

W I T N E S S E T H:

WHEREAS, First Parties together own the capital stock of the Compania Palomas de Terrenos y Ganado, S. A., hereinafter referred to as Cia. Palomas, having an outstanding capital stock of 17,500 shares of par value of 100.00 pesos each, of which 14,500 shares are owned by the Palomas Land and Cattle Company, and 3,000 shares are owned by the Hueco Cattle Company; and,

WHEREAS, said Cia. Palomas owns assets in Mexico, consisting principally of lands and cattle; and,

WHEREAS, Second Parties have proposed to form a corporation under the laws of the Republic of Mexico having the name of Nacional Ganadera, S. A. de C. V., having a minimum capitalization of 25,000.00 pesos, with its principal office at Ciudad Juarez, Chih., Mexico, and with appropriate powers, and to obligate such corporation to purchase from First Parties the entire capital stock of the Cia. Palomas for a total consideration of $1,000.000.00 in United States currency, payable as hereinafter set out, and to operate the ranch and properties of the Cia. Palomas through the means of such corporation so

-1-

217

-4-

The First Parties agree, promptly and prior to the close
of the sale of the Cia. Palomas stock as herein contemplated,
to do whatever may be necessary to cancel and remove all lia-
bilities from the books of the Cia. Palomas, except, however,
it is particularly understood and agreed that Second Parties
and the corporation to be formed, are accepting the stock
of the Cia. Palomas with full knowledge that there is, at
this time, litigation pending in the courts of Mexico relative
to the titles to the lands owned and held by Cia. Palomas, and
second parties and said corporation so to be formed shall accept such stock subject to such litigation and all claims of
any kind and character incidental or attendant thereto or growing out of the same, or otherwise, whether asserted therein or
not, and in this connection Second Parties shall immediately
take control, in the name of Cia. Palomas, of such litigation
and diligently attend to and prosecute the same and do everything within their power to protect the interests of the Cia.
Palomas in regard thereto.

Among the assets of Cia. Palomas is a claim for 34,398.65
pesos against the Republic of Mexico for certain lands sold
under a certain contract dated the 29th day of March, 1926,
which is hereby referred to. It is recognized that such asset
is of a very doubtful nature and First Parties make no repre-
sentation in regard thereto, and Second Parties accept the
same with full knowledge thereof, with the understanding that
they may, at their own expense, prosecute or settle the same
in any manner in which they may see fit.

Also listed as an asset of such company is an item of
5,064.95 pesos, which consists of (1) a claim for 1,500.00
pesos, representing a cash bond posted for Forest Law violation, and (2) a claim for 3,564.95 pesos, representing a
cash bond posted for possible additional 1938 Mexican income taxes. It is agreed that second parties, in the name
-6-

218

of Cia. Palomas, will diligently prosecute such claims to completion and deliver to First Parties any sums received by them.

It is also understood that 1939 and 1940 Mexican income taxes due by the Cia. Palomas have not been finally reviewed by the proper tax authorities. Any additional assessment shall be paid by First Parties. Any rebates received shall be delivered to First Parties.

First Parties obligate themselves to cancel a certain financing agreement existing between Husco Cattle Company and the Cia. Palomas and to relieve Cia. Palomas of and from any and all obligations imposed on it by such agreement.

It is understood and agreed that the Palomas Land and Cattle Company has prosecuted and is prosecuting a claim against the Mexican Government for cattle and other personal property formerly located on the Cia. Palomas ranch in Mexico, which was damaged and destroyed during the Mexican Revolution, in which claim Cia. Palomas has no interest and such claim and all rights and benefits accrued or to accrue therefrom are specifically retained by the Palomas Land and Cattle Company.

-5-

First Parties agree to promptly cause the cattle located on the lands of Cia. Palomas in Mexico to be rounded up so that an accurate count of all cattle on hand may be had. It is agreed (1) that representatives of both parties shall meet in Hachita, New Mexico, on the morning of February 28, 1941, (2) that the wagons shall start on the morning of March 1, 1941, and (3) that such count shall be effected in the most practical manner agreeable to both parties, taking into consideration weather conditions, range conditions, etc. Each animal counted shall be marked by clipping its tail, and all unbranded animals of weaning age shall be, at such time, branded. No 1941 calf shall be counted. At the time of taking the count mentioned, all old cows, which are to be se-

-7-

pleting the count, as previously detailed, and as and when such count is obtained, this sale shall be closed and possession given. In this connection, it is agreed that all current expenses, pensions, salaries of employees and all bills of the Cia. Palomas shall be paid by Cia. Palomas to date possession is delivered. First Parties further agree that the employment of all present employees of Cia. Palomas shall be terminated as of the date possession is granted, and no contracts of employment shall continue beyond such date. First Parties undertake to cause to be given all necessary notices in this connection and to pay all indemnity claims and expenses arising therefrom. It is also agreed that if any leases exist, they shall be terminated as of the date possession is granted.

Upon consummation of such sale and simultaneously with the delivery of possession, the books, records and files of the Cia. Palomas shall be delivered to Second Parties, with the exception of all abstracts and title papers to the lands belonging to Cia. Palomas, which shall be retained by First Parties until the consideration for the purchase of such stock, together with all interest thereon, is fully paid. At such time a representative of Second Parties shall inspect the abstracts and title papers covering the lands belonging to Cia. Palomas and First Parties shall make, execute and deliver to Second Parties a receipt for same, reciting that such instruments will be delivered to Second Parties as and when the purchase price, principal and interest is fully paid. First Parties also undertake to convey or cause to be conveyed to Ben F. Williams, one of Second Parties, by special warranty deed, the real estate, furniture, fixtures and office equipment in Columbus, New Mexico, now used as the office of the Rusco Cattle Company.

-9-

220

Should default be made in the payment of any install-
ment of principal and interest as it matures or should any
provision of this contract be violated or breached, then
and in any of said events the owners and holders of said notes
may accelerate the maturity thereof and declare the same immediately due and payable and proceed with such action as the
laws of either the United States or the Republic of Mexico
afford them, or any of them.

Any and all payments made on said notes shall be applied
first to the payment of interest to date of payment and
second to the principal thereof.

-7-

There shall be no personal liability on Second Parties
except as herein specifically set out.

IN WITNESS WHEREOF, said parties have hereunto signed
their names on the day and year first above written.

PALOMAS LAND AND CATTLE COMPANY

By: _____
        Vice-President.

ATTEST:

_____
Assistant Secretary.

HUECO CATTLE COMPANY

By: _____
        Vice-President.

ATTEST:

_____
Assistant Secretary.

FIRST PARTIES

_____
_____
_____
_____
_____

SECOND PARTIES.

221

BIBLIOGRAPHY

BOOKS

Arizona Historical Society. *Studies in Arizona History*. Tucson, Arizona, 1998.

Braddy, Haldeen. "The Head of Pancho Villa." *Western Folklore*, Vol. 119, No. 1 (Jan. 1960), pp. 25-33.

Buckley, F. Reid. *An American Family–The Buckleys.* New York: Threshold Editions, Simon & Schuster, 2008.

Christiansen, Larry D. "Bullets across the Border, Part I–The Situation and the Beginning." *Cochise County Quarterly*, Vol. 4, No. 4, December 1974.

_____. "Bullets across the Border, Part II–The Revolution Rekindled." *Cochise County Quarterly*, Vol. 5, No. 1, Spring 1975.

_____. "Bullets across the Border, Part III–Intrarevolutionary Troubles." *Cochise County Quarterly*, Vol. 5, No. 4, Winter 1975.

Cinefuegos, Ernesto. *La Voz de Aztlan*, June 22, 2007.

Cochise County Quarterly, Vol. 15, No. 4, Winter 1985.

De Fornaro, Carlo. *Carranza and Mexico.* New York: Mitchell Kennerly, 1915.

Douglas Daily International-American, September 1, 1914; October 29, 1915; November 3, 1915.

The Douglas Dispatch, A Photographic History of Douglas. Douglas, Arizona: Pediment Publishing, 2005.

Elías, Armando C., *Compendio de Datos Historicos de la Familia Elías.* Privately published, 1986.

_____. *Familia Elías, the Elías Family.* Privately published, 2008.

Erwin, Allen A. *The Southwest of John Horton Slaughter.* Spokane, Washington: The Arthur H. Clark Company, 1997.

Garfias, Luis M. *The Mexican Revolution, a Historic Politico-Military Compendium.* Col. Anzures, Mexico D.F.: Panorama Editorial, S.A., 1983.

Greenburg, Zack O. "Bones May Have Pancho Villa's Skull." *Yale Herald,* January 23, 2004.

Guzmán, Martín Luis. *Memoirs of Pancho* Villa. Austin, Texas: University of Texas Press, 1965.

Hall, Linda B. *Alvaro Obregón, Power and Revolution in Mexico, 1911-1920.* College Station, Texas: Texas A&M University Press, 1981.

Hall, Linda B., and Don M. Coerver. *Revolution on the Border, The United States and Mexico 1910-1920*. Albuquerque, New Mexico: University of New Mexico Press, 2008.

Harris III, Charles H. *The Secret War in El Paso*. Albuquerque, New Mexico: University of New Mexico Press, 2009.

Harris, Larry A. *Pancho Villa, Strong Man of the Revolution*. El Paso, Texas: The McMath Company, Inc., 1949.

Havemeyer, Loomis, Yale's Extracurricular & Social Organizations 1780 – 1960, Unpublished manuscript, January 1961.

Hayostek, Cindy. *Images of America: Douglas*. Charleston, S.C.: Arcadia Publishing, 2009.

Hurst, James W. *The Villista Prisoners of 1916-1917*. Las Cruces, New Mexico: Yucca Tree Press, September 2000.

Ibañez, V. Blasco. *The Four Horsemen of the Apocalypse*. New York: E.P. Dutton & Co., 1921.

_____. *Mexico in Revolution*. New York: E.P. Dutton & Company, 1920.

Irvin, Teresa Williams. *Let the Tail Go with the Hide, The Story of Ben F. Williams*. El Paso, Texas: Mangan Books, 1984.

Katz, Freiderich. *The Face of Pancho Villa, A History in Photographs and Words*. El Paso, Texas: Cinco Puntos Press, 1999.

_____. *The Life and Times of Pancho Villa*. Stanford, California: Stanford University Press, 1998.

Lansford, William Douglas. *Pancho Villa*. Los Angeles, California: Sherbourne Press, 1965.

Martinez, Oscar J. *Fragments of the Mexican Revolution: Personal Accounts from the Border*. Albuquerque, New Mexico: University of New Mexico Press, 1983.

McClintock, James H. *Mormon Settlement in Arizona*. Tucson, Arizona: University of Arizona Press, 1921.

Meed, Douglas V. *Bloody Border*. Tucson, Arizona: Westernlore Press, 1992.

_____. *Soldier of Fortune, Adventuring in Latin America and Mexico with Emil Lewis Holmdahl*. Houston, Texas: Halcyon Press, 2003.

Middagh, John. *Frontier Newspaper: The El Paso Times*. El Paso, Texas: Texas Western Press, 1958.

Naylor, Thomas H. "Massacre at San Pedro de la Cueva: The Significance of Pancho Villa's Disastrous Sonora Campaign." *The Western Historical Quarterly*, Vol. 8, No. 2 (April 1977), pp. 125-150.

Osorio, Rubén. *The Secret Family of Pancho Villa: An Oral History*. Alpine, Texas: Sul Ross State University, Center for Big Bend Studies, 2000.

Pérez, Marco Antonio Gómez. *Pancho Villa, El Dorado de la Revolución Mexicana*. Nicolás San Juan, Mexico, D.F.: Grupo Editorial Tomo, S.A., 2002.

Poniatowska, Elena. *Las Soldaderas, Women of the Mexican Revolution*. El Paso, Texas: Cinco Punto Press, 1999.

Ragsdale, Kenneth Baxter. *Wings over the Mexican Border: Pioneer Military Aviation in the Big Bend*. Austin, Texas: University of Texas Press, 1984.

Reed, John. *Insurgent Mexico*. Middlesex, England: Penguin Books Ltd., 1914.

Robbins, Alexandra. *Secrets of the Tomb*. Boston: Little, Brown & Company, September 2002.

Roca, Paul M. *Paths of the Padres through Sonora*. Tucson, Arizona: Arizona Pioneers Historical Society, 1967.

Romo, David Dorado. *Ringside Seat to a Revolution*. El Paso, Texas: Cincos Puntos Press, July 2005.

Rouverol, Jean. *Pancho Villa, A Biography*. Garden City, New York: Doubleday & Company, 1972.

Salas, Elizabeth. *Soldaderas in the Mexican Military*. Austin, Texas: University of Texas Press, 1990.

Singer, Mark. "La Cabeza de Villa." *New Yorker*, November 27, 1989.

_____. *Character Studies*. Boston: Houghton Mifflin Company, 2005.

Slattery, Matthew T. *Felipe Angeles and the Mexican Revolution*. Parma Heights, Ohio: Greenbriar Books, 1978.

Smith, Jr., Cornelius C. *Fort Huachuca: The Story of a Frontier Post*. Fort Huachuca, Arizona: Privately published, 1976.

Sutton, Anthony C. *America's Secret Establishmen: An Introduction to the Order of Skull and Bones*. Walterville, Oregon: Trine Day, 1983.

Tompkins, Colonel Frank. *Chasing Villa: The Last Campaign of the U.S. Cavalry*. Silver City, New Mexico: High-Lonesome Books, 1996.

Torres, Elias L. *La Cabeza de Villa*. El Libro Español, 1938.

Traywick, Ben T. *That Wicked Little Gringo*. Tombstone, Arizona: Red Marie's Bookstore, 2001.

Williams, Ben F. *Let the Tail Go with the Hide*. El Paso, Texas: Mangan Books, 1984.

NEWSPAPERS

Arizona Daily Star
Douglas Daily Dispatch
Douglas Daily International
El Paso Daily Times
El Paso Herald
El Paso Herald Post
El Paso Times
New York Times
Santa Fe New Mexican
Tucson Citizen
Washington, D.C. Evening Star

INTERVIEWS

Armando Elías, June 10, 2010.

Art Gaona, April 3, 2010.

INTERNET

www.footnote.com, historic documents, partnering with the National Archives, the Library of Congress, and other institutions.

ARCHIVAL COLLECTIONS

Arizona Historical Society, Tucson, Arizona

Bisbee Mining & Historical Museum Archives, Bisbee, Arizona

C.L. Sonninchsen Special Collections Department University of Texas at El Paso

Cochise County Historical Society, Douglas, Arizona

El Paso Public Library, Border Heritage Center Aultman Collection

Johnson Historical Museum of the Southwest, John Slaughter Ranch, Douglas, Arizona

INDEX

Symbols

A

B

LIST OF PHOTOS AND MAPS

Breinigsville, PA USA
22 November 2010
249819BV00003B/4/P